21 LEADERSHIP LESSONS

21 LEADERSHIP LESSONS

SUCCESSES, FAILURES, AND DISCOVERIES FROM A LIFE IN BUSINESS AND SPORTS

RICHARD PEDDIE

Library and Archives Canada Cataloguing in Publication Data

Peddie, Richard, 1947-, author
21 leadership lessons : successes, failures, and discoveries from a life in business and sports / Richard Peddie.

Includes index.
Issued in print and electronic formats.
ISBN 978-0-9939990-4-8 (bound).—ISBN 978-0-9939990-5-5 (html)

1. Leadership. I. Title. II. Title: Twenty-one leadership lessons.

HD57.7.P438 2015 658.4'092 C2015-905982-8
C2015-905983-6

Production Credits
Editor: Karen Milner
Interior design and typesetting: Adrian So
Cover design: Adrian So
Printer: Friesens

Published by Milner & Associates Inc.
www.milnerassociates.ca

Printed in Canada
10 9 8 7 6 5 4 3 2 1

This book is dedicated to the thousands of men and women I had the great fortune to work with over my career. When asked what I am most proud of, I have never hesitated to say that it was all the people whom I helped develop into very good leaders.

CONTENTS

“HE INSPIRES THE UNINSPIRED”

—Van Wilder, a character from the National Lampoon movie of the same name

FAQ

SO WHY SHOULD I BUY THIS BOOK?

Well, first of all I think it is damn good value. And I am confident that my leadership lessons can help you realize more career success. You will also discover things that you never thought about before. This book should make you think.

WHY DID YOU WRITE ANOTHER BOOK? I HEARD YOU SAY MANY TIMES ON RADIO THAT *DREAM JOB* WAS IT.

Yeah, I guess I was wrong. Not the first time and won't be the last. At the time I sure believed *Dream Job* would be the extent of my literary career, but as I talked to young leaders I thought I had more to offer and could help them get much better at leading people. So, like Coach Calipari at Kentucky, I loaded up again with a new crop of lessons and started writing again. Hmmm . . . now the question is, will I write a third book?

I AM DOING FINE IN MY JOB—WHY DO I NEED TO LEARN MORE ABOUT LEADERSHIP ?

If you aspire to being an excellent leader someday, your leadership journey is never done. I was a very successful leader at Pillsbury in 1989. However, if I had stayed the same leader, time would definitely have passed me by and I would never have had the business success or career I had at Maple Leaf Sports & Entertainment (MLSE), for example.

YOUR TEAMS DID NOT DO VERY WELL ON THE ICE, COURT, OR PITCH—WHY SHOULD I TAKE YOUR ADVICE?

You don't have to. But look at the companies I led and the success I had off the playing field. Things like launching new products, developing companies that were exceptional places to work, creating successful future leaders, and dramatically increasing enterprise value. If you want pure sports advice and success stories, read books about Jack Donohue or Phil Jackson. But if you want career leadership advice, this is a good read.

WHAT IS THE BEST WAY TO READ THIS BOOK AND APPLY THE LESSONS IN IT?

Actually, I would suggest there is no one best way. Unlike most books, the narrative in *21 Leadership Lessons* does not require that you read it in a linear fashion, starting with the first chapter and reading through it to the last. There are many leadership tips in the book. Some will interest you, some will not. Some you may have mastered already, some you may need to work on a bit to develop your skills in a particular area. Open up the table of contents and pick out the chapters that best describe the topics you are interested in and read those. As you move through your leadership journey you will find that there are lessons that may not interest you now but will apply to you a few years from now. This is a book you can easily dip into at any time and come away with some quick hits of leadership wisdom.

I HAVE QUICKLY THUMBED THROUGH YOUR BOOK AT A STORE AND I NOTICE THAT YOU USE A GYM BAG ANALOGY TO TELL YOUR STORY. WHAT DOES A GYM BAG HAVE TO DO WITH LEADERSHIP?

You will understand much better when you read the entire book (so spend your money and buy it). I am sure you had a gym bag or two as a kid. Over the years you put in and took out the things that you needed to play sports or go to the gym. Well, I think that a successful leader should have a leadership gym bag that they can take leadership lessons out of when they need them. In this book I have filled the gym bag with twenty-one key leadership lessons for you to think about.

I WANT TO HAVE A JOB IN SPORTS—WHAT IS YOUR ADVICE?

Run for cover. Seriously, if you cannot stand the heat from the fans and media, you should not even consider the sports business. Today, with social media, there is no place to hide and the spotlight can be exceptionally cruel. However, if you are still interested, "get your ticket punched" in all the areas that are important in the business of sports (I explain the concept of getting your ticket punched in a few chapters in the book, and in most detail in Lesson 3). And do something every day that moves you closer to your dream of a career in the sports industry.

WHAT IS THE ONE MOST IMPORTANT PIECE OF LEADERSHIP ADVICE YOU CAN GIVE ME?

Carefully read my chapters on "What" and "How." Vision and values have been the backbone of my leadership philosophy for most of my career. And, most importantly, they worked every time.

WHY DID YOU HIRE JOHN FERGUSON, JR.?

Sorry, this book is not about specifics like the hiring and firing of coaches and general managers on my watch. But it is about a leader doing their homework and making the best leadership decisions they can. What I will say is that John's résumé was excellent (player, scout, agent, worked in the NHL, VP with the St. Louis Blues, lawyer, family DNA, etc.); however, hiring him as the Leafs' GM did not work out, demonstrating that hiring is still a very imperfect art today.

I SEE YOU ADMIT TO FAILURES IN YOUR BOOK TITLE. WHY WOULD YOU EVER DO THAT?

Well, first of all, no leader is perfect. I made mistakes and I owned up to them. This gave me credibility with my employees and my bosses. It also made me more human and more humble. The important thing is that I tried to learn from each mistake, and I think mostly I did.

YOU RETIRED ALMOST FOUR YEARS AGO AND TODAY YOU

DON'T LEAD ANY COMPANIES ANYMORE, SO WHY ARE YOU STILL FOCUSING ON LEADERSHIP?

"*Ancora imparo*," as Michelangelo said—"I am still learning." They say what a leader knows pales in comparison to what he or she still doesn't know. I still love learning and keeping up with the changes in leadership as time goes by. I also enjoy teaching and mentoring young leaders, with the hope that I can help some of them realize their career dreams.

HOW DO I FIND A MENTOR?

You probably won't find one. Really good mentors are tough to find and, interestingly, they mostly gravitate to helping people who are already doing pretty well. So you will likely need to figure out how to be great leader without having a mentor. I never had a mentor either, so over my career I turned to books for help (and I share some of my favourites later in this book). I hope *21 Leadership Lessons* can be one of your mentors as you go through your career.

WILL THE LEAFS EVER WIN ANOTHER STANLEY CUP?

Okay, I will answer one sports question. I know it's been forty-eight years and counting for the Leafs, and, boy, did I get tired hearing about that over the years. Statistically the Leafs have a 3.3 percent chance over time to win their fourteenth Cup. If all of the investments MLSE has recently made in the Leaf management team work out, it could be as early as five years from now. But sports is really tough and full of smart, creative people all trying to win, so time will tell.

INTRODUCTION

PACKING YOUR GYM BAG

"NOPE. ONE AND DONE."

This was always my quick and consistent answer when someone asked me if I was ever going to write another book after *Dream Job*.

To answer that frequent question about writing another book, I constantly compared myself to the University of Kentucky Wildcats basketball team. Each year Kentucky has its star freshmen chase an NCAA championship for only one season before most of the players go pro. When it comes to attending university the kids are "one and done." And I thought the same would be true for me as an author, that one book would be enough. However, after speaking with numerous students and young leaders I became convinced that I wasn't "one and done" after all. That I still had another story to tell about how anyone aspiring to be successful in business should fill their metaphorical gym bag with leadership lessons.

Okay then, but why a gym bag analogy? I first used this analogy when I was teaching Elite Training at Maple Leaf Sports & Entertainment (from this point on MLSE). I figure that a long career is much like a workout, and winning in your career is much like winning in sports. So why not write about a gym bag full of instructive leadership lessons? This concept of putting lessons in a gym bag resonated with my Elite classes and, therefore, I thought it would resonate with you, too. So instead of putting new Nike socks into your gym bag, put in lessons about vision and values. Instead of putting the newest Bauer skates in your gym bag, fill it with things like best practices, contrary thinking, and optimism.

And why did I pick twenty-one as the number of lessons? Well, not because Borje Salming or Bobby Baun proudly wore that number for the Maple Leafs. And definitely not because Marcus Camby wore it for two half-hearted years with the Raptors. I chose twenty-one because I wrote this book for young leaders, and twenty-one years of age, in my mind, is a kind of jumping-off spot from youth to young adulthood. Also, today's young adults are going to grow up leading organizations through a twenty-first century that will be full of many new challenges and opportunities. In my experience, having a gym bag full of solid leadership lessons may help evolving leaders realize their dreams.

There is a concept that says we all have a personal narrative that shapes our view of the world and ourselves. My narrative is that I decided early in life that I wanted to be a student of leadership. I also realized quickly that for me to stay current and to continue to grow, my investment in leadership could never end. This book, *21 Leadership Lessons*, recounts the details of my personal leadership narrative. I know that it is far from perfect, but it has worked tremendously well for me. I hope much of what I have written works for you, too.

LESSON 1

WHAT? THE IMPORTANCE OF HAVING A VISION

ONE DAY YOU WRITE DOWN A DREAM and it changes your life. A few years later you read a bestselling book and it completely changes how you lead. Along the way you realize that your dream will not come true unless you invest in becoming a better leader.

During my leadership journey all of these three things happened to me. In the first instance, I was studying business administration at the University of Windsor. At the time, Windsor was a hotbed of men's university basketball (today both the men and women kick ass) and I loved the game. But, knowing with absolute certainty that no on-court pro career awaited me, I decided that my dream would be to run an NBA franchise one day. In 1967 that was a very ambitious dream as there were only twelve NBA teams in existence, and none of them was in Canada. Toronto actually had one of the very first NBA franchises. The Toronto Huskies played in the old Maple Leaf Gardens for one year during the 1946-47 season and, after a 22-36 win-loss record, quickly disbanded.

At the time I first had my basketball dream I did something else really important—I wrote my dream down in a journal that I was keeping. Years later I would come across research proving that if a person has a dream (or a vision, or objective) and writes it down, they have a significantly better chance of realizing their dream than someone who does not.

"If a person has a dream and writes it down, they have a significantly better chance of realizing their dream than someone who does not."

Fourteen years later, then a rookie president at Hostess Foods, I would read the book *In Search of Excellence*, and it convinced me that having a clear corporate vision and values could help a company be more successful. I then used the authors' suggested approach in three different companies and it worked very well with each of them.

Lastly, I invested continuously in making my dream come true by studying leadership voraciously and getting my ticket punched in three different industries. That experience not only helped me eventually attain my dream job as president of the Toronto Raptors and then of MLSE, but my investment in my own leadership development ultimately enabled me to realize long-term business success. Note that I specifically said "business success," because during my tenure at MLSE we generated excellent business results that increased enterprise value six times over, to two billion dollars, although we had no real success on the ice, court, or pitch. I don't believe, as some have intimated, that our focus on vision and values at MLSE was a distraction that somehow detracted from the performance of our sports franchises. Simply put, I—along with our owners, our general managers, coaches, scouts, and players—did not get the job done with any of our teams.

• • ● • •

Over the years I read and studied some vision statements that were way too long. Our vision statements at both Pillsbury and SkyDome were very effective, but I always thought they were still way too long for people to really remember them. MLSE'S vision and values statement was very easy to remember, at only eighteen words:

Win
Excite our fans
Inspire our people
Dedicated to our teams
Leaders in the community
Passion. Pride. Performance.

Interestingly, when I taught at MLSE I often asked our employees to write down our vision statement from memory, and every time I did 100 percent of the staff knew it word for word.

• • • • •

With our vision to "WIN," our driving goal was to do that both on and off the playing field. Win championships with our four teams, and win off the playing field by growing both profits and enterprise value. Our four values addressed our fans, employees, teams and community. When Tim Leiweke took over as MLSE's chief executive officer he claimed the company did not have a vision to win. But he was very mistaken! Yes, we were not winning on the playing field, but I knew that we had a clear winning vision off the playing field. From our positive research on employee attitudes, from walking the talk, and from comparing our financial metrics with all the teams in the NBA, MLS, and NHL, I clearly knew that our business results and our people were winners off the playing field.

Upon joining MLSE, Leiweke also boldly claimed he was going to bring a winning culture to the teams. He said the Leafs were "close," but on his watch the team registered only eighty-four points in the 2013-14 season and sixty-eight points in

2014-15, easily missing the playoffs both years. And, after spending about $100 million on new TFC player signings, in 2013 he confidently predicted football success (by the way, you'll notice that I always refer to "the beautiful game" as football, not soccer): "Mark it down, write it down, film it . . . we're going to turn around TFC and we're going to make the playoffs." Instead, TFC's payroll became easily the highest in Major League Soccer and the team finished thirteenth, once again out of the playoffs. Ironically, Leiweke's broken crystal ball said that the Raptors were a work in progress. But then he did make a wise decision by signing GM Masai Ujiri, and Masai did a smart thing re-signing coach Dwane Casey.

Leiweke's failure at MLSE reminded me of a story I once heard. It seems two presidents were talking about the progress they were making with their corporate vision and values. One president asked the other how he was doing. The other president said, "I don't know yet; I have only been at it for five years." The point here is that it is easy to make bold vision statements, but it is especially hard to deliver on them; and it takes a long time to build them into the DNA of the company. And as I will talk about in Lesson 18, it is tough to win it all in business and even tougher to do it in sports.

> **"It's easy to make bold vision statements, but it is especially hard to deliver on them."**

• • • • •

A winning vision statement is a compelling, reinforcing, inspiring statement of intent—something seen in a dream even. Astronaut Chris Hadfield said that a good dream has to be a real stretch: "Give yourself a dream right on the edge of possible." I think short, inspirational vision statements are best. Like the one The Princess Margaret Cancer Centre has, "To conquer cancer in our lifetime," or Disney's original mission statement, "Make people happy."

Or there are the very personal dreams that are not written down, but an effective driving force just the same. For instance, basketball player Muggsy Bogues was never, ever going to be more than five-foot-three-inches tall, but he still wanted to play in the NBA, where the average player height was sixteen inches taller at six-foot-seven. Despite his severe height handicap, Muggsy had a solid college career at Wake Forest, was taken twelfth in the draft, and went on to have a successful fourteen-year career in the NBA. He made up for his height handicap by being an exceptional passer and one of the fastest players on the court. It was fun to have him with the Raptors at the end of his career.

When I decided to get involved in the 2014 Toronto mayoral race as a co-chair of Olivia Chow's mayoral campaign, I really tried to convince Chow and her team to come up with an inspiring vision for Toronto. She did come up with some excellent initiatives on transit, after-school programs, job creation for youth, and more; but her messaging never laddered up to a succinct, clearly articulated vision statement that turned voters in her direction. I will never know if that lack of a grand vision for the city of Toronto contributed to her defeat, but I am convinced that the lack of it did not help. Interestingly, neither of the Fords (Rob or Doug) nor John Tory articulated a truly cohesive vision for the city, but one won and the other came closer than many believed possible just the same.

Once, when I was pushing Chow's team on the need to create a vision for Toronto, one of her staff asked me, "But will it work in politics?" I told him it had worked for me in three companies and I could point to lots of other companies where it had worked as well. I also quoted an article in the *Harvard Business Review* where professor Rosabeth Moss Kanter talks about how great companies think differently. Here is her quote, but I have replaced the word companies with cities: "The first step is getting behind a common vision. Top leaders exemplify and communicate the [city's] purpose and values, but everyone owns them, and the values become embedded in tasks, goals and performance standards." Still, I had no luck convincing Olivia's team. So if I ever want to prove or disprove my theory that having a vision will work in politics, I guess I will just have to find a mayoral candidate who wants to give it a go in 2018.

As I read about and practiced having a personal or corporate vision, I began to accumulate a list of tangible pluses that come from having one. In no particular order, here are a few key advantages of defining a clear vision:

- Makes it clear to everyone WHAT you or your company want to be, WHAT you want to accomplish.
- Gives you or your organization a unique purpose.
- Explains to others the enduring purpose of the organization.
- Brings a focus to the allocation of resources.

- Helps speed up decision making.
- Makes a company more resilient during the inevitable bad times. I know MLSE's vision and values helped our employees safely navigate through a couple of ugly work stoppages in the NHL and NBA.

• • • • •

To make sure that the vision is successfully driven deep into your organization, it is important that it is rock solid and does not drift with the trends and fashions of the day. MLSE's vision and values hardly changed over fourteen years and, therefore, became deeply engrained into our corporate culture. After I retired, however, they were changed twice in less than two years, which likely presents a number of challenges to leadership and employees alike. Frequently chopping and changing something as fundamental as your vision or values statement can be confusing, disruptive, and may mean the vision and values are not followed at all. Your vision and values statements should be a beacon for the organization, a moral compass that remains constant and consistent over time.

"Your vision and values statements should be a beacon for the organization, a moral compass that remains constant and consistent over time."

When I heard that MLSE's original vision and values had not survived my retirement, I expressed my disappointment to a past vice president of the company, Beth Robertson. Beth made me feel a little better when she told me, "They live in the people that worked for you and they shaped them as leaders." Thanks, Beth.

Today, a leadership approach that emphasizes vision and values is not as popular in organizations as it once was. There are still a number of leading companies that practice the theory very well, but there are more that either do it very badly or do not do it at all. And one can easily find a number of voices that will tell you that vision and values are just a soft and cuddly waste of time.

For example, author David Axson comes down hard on vision statements, dismissing them as being "a long awkward sentence that demonstrates management's inability to think clearly." Well, that definitely hasn't been my experience and, because they have been so central to my career success, Vision and Values are the first two lessons in this book. This Japanese proverb sums up nicely just how important I think they are to leadership success: "A vision without action is a daydream; action without a vision is a nightmare."

LESSON 2

HOW? VALUES TURN VISION INTO ACTION

CREATING A CORPORATE VISION STATEMENT is pretty easy. You can quickly create it yourself. You can get a group of people together to create it. You can even pay a consulting firm lots of money to write it for you. Then you can immediately do simple things like calling a big staff meeting to announce it, put posters up to display it on every wall, and brag about it in your annual report. Like I said, pretty easy.

> **"To realize your corporate or personal vision, you have to define and articulate your chosen values as well."**

Creating a personal vision statement is entirely up to you and is dependent on you first deciding what you want to achieve in your career. But to ever actually realize your corporate or personal vision you have to define and articulate your chosen values as well. Values are HOW an individual or an organization realizes a dream.

Your values, and the statement that encapsulates them, have to be solid and they must reflect the way you and everyone in your organization thinks, acts, talks, in every way, every day. You can't just follow these values when it is convenient and more profitable to do so. Actually, your values become most powerful when it is inconvenient and more expensive to follow them. For instance, when a big personal or business issue comes along (and during your career this is sure to happen), clear values will point you in the right direction. Pursuing the path that is right for you or your business is not always easy, but values will, in effect, serve as the moral compass for all to follow.

There should be no time-outs. Values are the qualities on which a company or an individual should depend. They are the rules of the game, and while your strategies and tactics need to change with the times, core values do not.

Just like having a vision has real tangible benefits, so does having a few core values:

- They make clear to your staff HOW you are going to realize your dream.
- Like your vision, they also cause a more focused allocation of resources. Resources, such as people and dollars, are not infinite; you have to spend your limited money and time on what delivers your vision most effectively.
- Values are standards or principles that guide behaviour and empower employees to self-regulate instead of be micro-managed. One of MLSE's values was, "Excite every fan." We did not define exactly what that meant—we left that for our employees to figure out. This type of empowerment liberated our people to do the right things by our fans and corporate partners.
- They give your employees a clear sense of direction as opposed to having them wonder what is important to the company. If a company values things like high quality, great service, and innovation, the employees know this is what is expected of them. Every spring at MLSE our employees received a written performance evaluation. The first section in the formal evaluation was always how they were doing at living our vision and values.
- And finally, if a company sticks with its values, those core principles become an excellent compass for years to come. Over time, a company is absolutely sure to be tested, and

if its values are true, they will help the company make the right decision. When I ran Pillsbury–Green Giant we once had a multimillion-dollar decision to make on product quality; but it was actually an easy, albeit expensive, decision because of one of the company's core values, "quality is essential." Despite the potential negative impact on everyone's bonus, the entire team quickly agreed that we could not sell the product.

• • • • •

Through the years I have seen a number of effective company values. Values like quality, service, and innovation show up quite a bit. Actually, I do not think it matters exactly what your values are as long as they are positive values, you give them a lot of thought when you choose them, and, most importantly, you always live by them.

Having a "people" value is really common. Frankly I cannot imagine an organization not having one. Pillsbury had one that I have personally adopted for my own use to this day: "people make the difference" (I talk about that idea in more detail in Lesson 4). In addition to Pillsbury, SkyDome and MLSE also had a "people" value under my watch. After I left MLSE, their new president, Tom Anselmi, changed the company's vision and values statement and dropped the "inspire our people" value. Tom explained to me that he only "tweaked" the statement and that the importance of people was so obvious the company did not have to

> **"I cannot imagine an organization not having a 'people' value."**

mention it any longer. I disagreed and every MLSE employee I talked to about it was disappointed about its absence. Employees were left with the impression that they were important for fourteen years but for some reason they weren't important any longer.

Again, try to be as constant with your values as possible for consistency and continuity. These principles are at the core of your corporate culture and they define who you are and how you behave as an organization; they shouldn't waver and change on a whim.

• • • • •

Authentic personal values are key to being a great leader, but it's also best that your personal values be a close reflection of the values held by your boss and the company. Over my career I have seen many people struggle with the fact that their values do not align with the company they work for. Many of those people had to leave the company because they could not reconcile the differences. Unfortunately some chose to compromise their personal values in order to keep their job. Others actually changed their personal values to fit with the company. When people do that, it says to me that their personal values were not very authentic to begin with.

When Muggsy Bogues played for the Raptors I never thought to ask him what his personal values were, and I doubt very much if he ever wrote them down; but I know he had them just the same. If I were to guess, I'd say Muggsy's first value would be "perseverance," for sticking with his NBA dream. Next, "team player," as witnessed by the eight assists per game he averaged throughout his career; "high energy," as demonstrated by the speed at which he always played the game; and finally "passion," manifested in the obvious joy he demonstrated on and off the court. Muggsy's NBA dream and values helped him leave a positive mark wherever he put on a uniform.

Muggsy realized his dream with the help of his own core values. On the flip side there is Lance Armstrong, a spectacular example of horrible personal values. Armstrong, a professional road racing cyclist, had a dream to win the Tour de France, and he won it a record seven consecutive times! However, over the years there were repeated rumours that he was using drugs to succeed. Knowing that he had successfully beaten testicular cancer, often fatal, I did not want to believe the rumours and rooted for him when he competed in every Tour. But then I learned, along with the rest of the world, that after a full investigation the USDA concluded that Armstrong had conducted "the most sophisticated, professionalized and successful doping program that sport has ever seen." He was stripped of all his medals and banned from competing for life.

Clearly Armstrong had a compelling and inspiring dream; but his personal values left a lot to be desired. To win, he embraced cheating, lying, and intimidation. It's interesting that Armstrong still hasn't learned from his history of lying and cheating. Early in 2015, he was driving after having a few drinks, and crashed into a couple of parked cars. But instead of owning up to the truth, he had his partner lie and say that she did it. The police found out and once again Armstrong was caught lying. I guess when you have bad values you always have bad values.

In *The Globe and Mail*, columnist Cathal Kelly condoned drug use by athletes, reasoning that they are primarily "entertainers." He believed the use of drugs was not a morally bad thing, just "a compromise in order to smooth the path." After reading the article, I immediately tweeted out my criticism of his column. Kayaker Adam van Koeverden, winner of Olympic gold, silver, and bronze medals for Canada, went one better by writing an articulate rebuttal from a clean athlete's point of view. I liked how van Koeverden related Armstrong's cheating back to Kelly's own profession of journalism: "If cheating is so easily justified, how far would a journalist go to achieve their goals? Is it ok to plagiarize for a Pulitzer Prize? Lie for a front page? Misquote someone for a racy exposé?" Well, Kelly, how do you answer that question? I know where I stand.

Like Muggsy, I never wrote down my personal values either, but over time I realized that my own core values—such as curiosity, optimism, courage, and authenticity—definitely dictate HOW I lead. Curiosity drove my interest in reading, walking the talk, and developing best practices. Optimism fuelled my belief that one day I could run a basketball team and, over the years, positively influenced almost every business decision I ever made. I am no fighter, but I had the courage to stand up for what I believed was right, and the courage to admit my fallibility when I was wrong. And, finally, I believe I am authentic; what you see with Richard Peddie is what you get.

When I joined Pillsbury they had just launched their vision and values statement but I was very comfortable with it because it talked to the importance of people, quality, and excellence in everything we did. When I moved on to lead SkyDome and

MLSE, I was one of the authors of the statements, so I ensured that the corporate values aligned with my personal ones. Unless you attain a very senior position in a company you may never get a chance to help author a corporate vision and values statement. However, to have personal success and to remain with the company, you personally will have to be aligned with whatever direction the company chooses.

• • • • •

In his book, *Built to Last*, Jim Collins has identified a number of companies with strong vision and values. A few of my favourites are Disney, GE, and Four Seasons. While his book does identify several companies that compare less favourably to his top eighteen, he does not discuss in any detail any companies that exhibit horrible values. And, believe me, they are out there. There are far too many organizations in which discrimination, price fixing, environmental infractions, or unsafe work environments are commonplace. Whether these corporate citizens are simply turning a blind eye to unacceptable behaviour or actively condoning it, they are not living by positive organizational values and are usually toxic places to work.

“Organizations that turn a blind eye to unacceptable behaviour or actively condone it are usually toxic places to work.”

When people ask me for advice on a company they are thinking about working for, I encourage them to look very closely at not only what companies may *say* about their vision and values on their website and in their annual report, but also, and more importantly, to look at how they are actually living by them—how they *act* on their stated vision and values. For example, what corporate decisions they are making? How do they treat their employees and the communities they operate in? If you have real trouble getting the lowdown on a company's values, talk to some of their employees to get the inside dope. It is important that you have a job where you can continue to follow your dream and to work for a company with values that align with your own.

There are two organizations that practice values that I have real issues with. One is Walmart. The largest company by revenue in the United States, with an enterprise value of approximately $260 billion dollars. On the positive side, they employ two million people in 11,767 stores, in twenty-seven countries. They are an anchor tenant in many malls and their low prices save shoppers a lot of money. And in 2015 they are going to invest $340 million in new Canadian facilities. So I want to believe they are a good company, but I simply cannot get there. Their litany of bad behaviour just wears on me.

From using bribery in Mexico to get the store locations they want; to being the largest seller of guns and ammunition in the United States, their business practices leave much to be desired, in my opinion. Over the years, they have also faced numerous allegations of salary discrimination for paying their almost 900,000 female employees significantly less than they pay their male employees. They had to pay a $110 million fine in California for dumping hazardous waste. And, sorry, their recent move in the United States to increase wages to all of nine dollars an hour simply doesn't begin to cut it. Like I said, there is much to like about Walmart, but to me their values in action are still seriously lacking. I would like to remind them of what Peter Parker, the alter-ego of the comic character Spider-Man, once said: "With great power comes great responsibility."

Now, I cannot for the life of me begin to defend my next example of an organization that exhibits horrible values in action: Florida State University (FSU). Actually, it's not difficult these days to find a major NCAA program that has lost its way and is putting the "athlete" way ahead of the "student athlete," sacrificing academic ideals for pure financial gain. The drive to win, fill stadiums, sign larger sponsorship deals, negotiate huge broadcast agreements, and generally make alumni happy so they'll give funds generously to their *alma mater* is well beyond the tipping point on too many U.S. campuses. From the Sandusky scandal at Penn State, to giving out phoney grades to athletes at the University of North Carolina and Syracuse University, to paying coaches millions of dollars, to spending more on athletic facilities than classrooms—many university presidents are looking the wrong way in their drive to win.

Many days I think some of the big U.S. schools have lost their minds and, worse, have completely forgotten their original purpose. For two years I was on the board of directors for Canadian Interuniversity Sport (CIS). The board oversees athletics for all of Canada's universities, and was convinced that Canada's fifty-plus universities have the right student-athlete balance. However, I still cautioned board members and athletic directors against getting caught up in wanting to win above anything else, and forgetting their real role is to help graduate awesome, well educated, well rounded young adults.

In my mind, FSU is among the worst schools in the NCAA in terms of their behaviour and their values in action, and their biggest offender is their nationally ranked football program. Whether it's their coach, athletic director, university president, alumni, or the Tallahassee police department, they have all let their young men get way with unacceptable behaviour for many years, in some cases with crimes literally and figuratively close to murder. During his time at the school, their star receiver, Aaron Hernandez, assaulted a waiter, failed multiple drug tests, and shot up a passing automobile. For all this he should have faced bans for up to half a season, but he did not miss a single snap. And why am I not surprised that he was eventually indicted for the murder of Odin Lloyd by a U.S. grand jury in 2013?

Unfortunately, Hernandez was not the only problem athlete at FSU. In 2014, one of FSU's star cornerbacks drove into an oncoming car, totalling both vehicles. Rather than remaining at the scene, he fled, leaving his car in the middle of the street. The police responded and cooperated with the Florida State University police. By the next day it was as if the hit-and-run had never happened. Over the years the university and the local police have gone easy on FSU football players.

One of the more high-profile examples was the almost complete lack of police investigation into a 2012 rape accusation against quarterback Jameis Winston, who would actually go on to win the Heisman Trophy in 2013. The university did not even get around to conducting a disciplinary hearing in the Winston case until almost two years after the accusation was made. Despite shouting crude obscenities in the student union and being caught shoplifting, Winston was suspended for only one meaningless game, and the university only did that because there was so much public outcry. I do love the fact that despite a very good year on the field, Winston's off-field behaviour likely caused him to not even make the short list for the 2014 Heisman trophy.

Interestingly, Winston performed the predictable "I know I made a mistake . . . I have to earn your trust" PR tour at the 2015 NFL combine. The man is now clearly trying to distance himself from his Tallahassee baggage. Unfortunately the NFL ignored his tainted past and, true to form, drafted him first overall, making him a very rich young man.

In 2014 the police turned over to the media 300 police reports linking FSU athletes to various crimes and misdemeanours. In one article, a writer from *The New York Times* concluded this about the FSU football program: "a team that doesn't have to follow the rules as long as it keeps winning." In my mind, FSU may exhibit among the worst values of any institution in the United States. Their president, John Thrasher, should be so proud!

• • • • •

Now, unfortunately I can't end this lesson by telling you that leaders with bad values always fail, because some do pretty well, at least for a while. How you conduct yourself is up to you. As a leader, do you want to lead with values that treat your customers, community, and employees fairly and honestly; or do you want to be that selfish leader who leads only for their own benefit? As a leader, it is your choice.

LESSON 3

GET YOUR TICKET PUNCHED

IF YOU HAVE DECIDED ON A DREAM industry or specific job that you really feel passionate about, you have to go about doing everything you can to make it happen. From getting the right education, to working in areas that give you the right experience, active networking, to even reading and studying about the job constantly. I refer to that as "getting your ticket punched," or marking a career milestone at every step of your personal leadership journey. And that's exactly what I did to realize my dream of leading an NBA team one day.

If you ever read my résumé, you would think I strategically planned every one of my career moves to make sure that I would realize my NBA dream. In part that was true. Although I didn't directly seek a job in the NBA at every stage of my career, every role I took on in some way prepared me for that eventual goal. In the early years, I was lucky enough to land positions that gave me excellent experience relevant to many industries; and as I continued on my career journey, I consciously chose to take on roles that would prepare me for my ultimate dream job.

"Every role I took on in some way prepared me for that eventual goal."

My early university years working for Air Canada in sales and customer service helped prepare me for running customer facing businesses like entertainment centres. My nineteen years in consumer products were priceless: Working at Colgate, General Foods, Hostess, and Pillsbury taught me about brands, marketing, sales, operations, finance, and helped develop my early leadership skills.

Moving on to SkyDome taught me how to run a sports facility, working with sports teams like the Blue Jays and Argos; promoting rock concerts; selling suites, food and beverage, and merchandise. Interestingly, the headhunter handling the SkyDome search asked why I should even be considered for the job, since I had absolutely had no sports facility experience; I told him that I believed the disciplines of consumer products could be successfully applied to the entertainment business. SkyDome was a very strategic move on my part. I knew having experience operating a sports facility would be a huge asset in working with a pro basketball franchise.

During the last year I worked at SkyDome, I had the good fortune to meet Larry Tanenbaum and head up his bid for an NBA expansion team. Unfortunately our Palestra group lost out, but I made a lot of excellent NBA contacts and gained some valuable basketball learning. It turned out that Palestra's failing was also fortuitous because it led me to the role of president and COO with NetStar, the company that at the time owned TSN, RDS, Discovery Channel, and Dome Productions. In that role I learned about live sports production, negotiating broadcast agreements, sports news reporting, and I even helped launch Canada's first sports website, TSN.ca.

Then on November 26, 1996, after twenty-nine years of getting my ticket punched, Allan Slaight offered me the job of president and CEO of the NBA's Toronto Raptors. I had done such a good job getting prepared for this opportunity, probably only Paul Beeston was more qualified in Canada for the role than I was.

Years later, I realized that I was just following the same formula recommended by Jack Canfield, author of *Chicken Soup for the Soul*: "Decide what it is you want. Write it down. Review it constantly. And each day do something that moves you towards that goal."

Today, I often have young leaders ask me for advice when they are considering a potential career move. Here are the questions I ask them in reply:

- What is your dream?
- What do you want to accomplish during your career?
- How does the new job you are considering move you in that direction? Or is it only a lateral move that will pay you a few bucks more?

My final advice is to work hard to get your ticket punched. Along the way you are likely to receive many job offers. But don't just drift from opportunity to opportunity, no matter how good the chance of promotion or how attractive the salary. Always have your final destination—your dream—in mind, and make purposeful, strategic choices about the path you take to get there.

LESSON 

PMTD: PEOPLE MAKE THE DIFFERENCE

PILLSBURY WAS THE FIRST COMPANY I LED that followed a real vision and values approach. Over my four years as president, my entire management team was completely dedicated to operating the company true to our collective vision and values. And the remarkable results we generated absolutely convinced me that this was the right way to go if I wanted to lead a successful company.

As I mentioned earlier, one of Pillsbury's three core values was "people make the difference." As I learned to say: Good people make good differences; great people make great differences; and not so good people either make no difference or, at times, can actually make a very bad difference. I think I had started to appreciate the importance of people while at Colgate, General Foods, and Hostess; but it was at Pillsbury where it became one of my twenty-one leadership lessons learned.

Just before I left Hostess Foods (the snack company that was ultimately acquired by Frito Lay) to join Pillsbury, I sat down with my best vice president, the late Stu Cairns. When I joined Hostess two years earlier, Stu was a hard guy to win over. He was a lifelong snack-foods guy and I was a "marketing weenie" from the parent company, General Foods. But Stu took the time to teach me the snack business, and in turn I worked very hard to learn it. On my last night at Hostess he turned the tables and gave me an employee exit evaluation. Over dinner, we discussed many leadership lessons learned, but the one thing he said that really stuck in my head was, "You didn't surround

"You can judge the quality of a business team by what they go on to do after they leave your company."

yourself with the best people. You should have made changes in a couple of the senior roles." I knew Stu spoke the truth.

When I made the move to Pillsbury I immediately upgraded marketing and plant leadership by hiring proven executives from General Mills and Procter & Gamble, respectively, and I replaced my CFO with a solid individual from the U.S. parent company. We also worked hard to develop the rest of the team by using a semi-annual corporate engineering exercise. The senior management team would meet and review all the company's middle managers to identify who was strong, who needed further development, and who needed to be replaced. I took this discipline to both SkyDome and MLSE and had success in each instance.

They say that you can judge a university by the quality of their alumni. I also think that you can judge the quality of a business team by what they go on to do after they leave your company. At least eight of the Pillsbury team went on to run their own businesses, and three of those individuals led much larger businesses than I ever ran.

At Pillsbury, SkyDome, and MLSE I worked hard to surround myself with a top-notch staff. A couple of times we hired poorly and the individual had to be let go. Sometimes an individual could not keep up with the growth or evolution of the company and we had to phase them out. But generally we had success attracting, developing, and motivating employees; unleashing their unique talents; and, most importantly, retaining the best of them.

I didn't think that was always the case with the coaching staffs of our sports teams at MLSE. On a couple of occasions,

I believed the head coach could have surrounded himself with much better assistants, for example. The owner of the Golden State Warriors also suggested that their head coach, Mark Jackson, was guilty of that same thing. I often wondered if coaches didn't always go for the best hire because they tended instead to bring in individuals who were longtime friends; or whether they lacked confidence and worried that if one of their assistants was too good he might one day replace him as head coach. There are many reasons why coaches, business leaders, and others don't always surround themselves with the most talented people or the best people for the job, but they should.

"Leaders don't always surround themselves with the most talented people or the best people for the job, but they should."

• • • • •

I am convinced that great people make a great difference. As far as I can determine, the first leader to say, "Employees are our most important asset" was an individual way back in the 1940s. Today, a more accurate phrase would be, "Talent is a business's greatest asset." Unfortunately, whichever way you choose to express that people make the difference and are your "most important asset," the way some leaders treat their people belies that statement entirely.

I recall in particular two conversations that brought the whole "people asset" thing to life for me. When the Maple Leafs bought the Raptors, I had a contract that allowed me to quit the company if I wished and still get a significant severance package. (Kind of like what Buffalo Bills head coach Doug Marrone had in his contract, only his 2015 payout was much larger than mine.) When it was time to renegotiate a new MLSE contract with Bob Bertram of the Ontario Teachers' Pension Plan, I asked for the same kind of clause to be included. Bob said he couldn't do that because when Teachers' ultimately sold MLSE, I would be viewed as one of the assets they were selling. I understood that!

Another time, I was talking to former MLSE board member, John McIntyre, about how companies treat the management team of the company they are acquiring. He said that his company, Birch Hill Equity Partners, views the acquired company's employees as important assets and they will do everything they can to keep and motivate the good ones. Unfortunately, I have also seen too many examples of corporate takeovers where the acquiring company doesn't take this approach at all, and will terminate or financially short-change the existing staff if they can get away with it.

When I retired from MLSE, I personally handed out a bottle of wine, packaged in a nice pine box, to each of our employees. Inscribed on the box was this quote from American novelist Brian Andrews: "Someday the light will shine like a sun through my skin and they will say, 'What have you done with your life?' And though there are many moments, I think I will remember in the end that I will be proud to say, 'I was one of us.'" I did this to say thanks personally to my team, and to recognize that we could not have accomplished all that we did at MLSE without a total team effort.

During your career you are sure to have a team of people reporting to you. Initially it may be only one or two, but as you become more senior it could be tens or hundreds and if you become a vice president or president it may be thousands. You may think you can do a lot by yourself. You are smart, creative, and work hard. But today things are just too difficult and too competitive to ever succeed all by yourself. As a leader, you will have to work hard to build the very best team you can. And you have to understand fundamentally that great people really will make a positive difference in your career.

So my PMTD lesson is one of the most important leadership lessons for you in this book.

LESSON 5

EMBRACE CONTRARY THINKING

HOW OFTEN DO YOU GET SILENTLY PEEVED or visibly upset when others challenge your thinking or believe their idea is better than yours? Well, get used to it because contrary points of view from people you work with are going to come your way all through your career, and how you respond to that input is going to help determine how successful a leader you will become.

It isn't always easy to listen to a contrary point of view. As a leader you think you are pretty smart, have done your homework, maybe even have come up with what you believe is a very creative idea; and then a boss, peer, or even a subordinate challenges you. I know that during my career I was sometimes guilty of not being as open-minded as I should have been when my ideas were challenged. My reaction over the years varied from being pretty defensive to completely ignoring the feedback. However, as I became more experienced, confident, and probably a little wiser, I became comfortable with being challenged. And started to recognize that being open to contrary thinking was key to having more personal and corporate success.

I think Ruth Simmons, the past president of Brown University and the first African-American president of an Ivy League school, said it best as part of a commencement address at Smith College, "One's voice grows stronger in encounters with opposing views." Add to that my belief that one's entire enterprise grows stronger when it listens to opposing views. Now, I am not talking about being bogged down by the pessimists, nor advising you not to take chances that

> **"As a leader, it is incumbent on you to encourage everyone in your organization to speak up and speak out."**

some more timid people will always try to talk you out of. No, I am talking about creating an environment that encourages people to speak up—to be contrary thinkers.

At MLSE, the best contrarian was my EVP, General Counsel, Robin Brudner. Robin is a hard working, committed leader; she's very bright and has high personal standards. She was the best on my team at always looking out for our fans and employees, especially if it looked like we were going to wander off the path of our corporate values. Robin and I often duked it out over ideas and decisions the company was contemplating. She was forceful, often stubborn, and you could never accuse her of not taking author and Facebook COO Sheryl Sandberg's advice to "lean in."

Over the years Robin and I had many sessions where we strongly debated issues and opportunities. Sometimes I agreed with her. Sometimes she convinced me to modify my point of view. And other times I said "no" and stuck to my decision. In all cases I heard her out and we worked effectively together. Robin once told me that her confidence to speak up came from my willingness to listen to her.

As a leader, it is incumbent on you to encourage everyone in your organization to speak up and speak out. This is where good ideas and continuous improvement come from, and this is one way to appreciate and nurture your employees by always making room for their contribution. And even if someone else's way of thinking doesn't make you change your mind on a particular issue, don't you think that you personally, and the enterprise as a whole, will have arrived at a better, more informed decision for it having been challenged?

• • • • •

Some things are very difficult to speak up about, such as unethical behaviour. This is especially true if you are a subordinate "speaking truth to power." But those are the things that a leader definitely must hear. Unethical behaviour, like sexual and racial harassment, cheating, and misuse of company funds, can completely destroy the culture of a company if it is not addressed.

Most major companies have put in confidential phone lines where people can anonymously call in their concerns. While this concept looks great on paper, these whistleblowing hotlines are almost always ineffective. Employees either don't trust the anonymity of their call or do not believe leadership will take action. The only way leaders will really know what is going on within a company is if they have established a culture where speaking out is encouraged and, more importantly, listened to.

> **"The conflict that arises from contrary thinking is just energy that simply needs to be managed."**

Unfortunately, a few times I have seen companies and weaker leaders not being able to accept their contrary thinkers, and instead pushing them out of the company. This unwillingness to listen to differing opinions and ideas scares off anyone else who was thinking about challenging policies or decisions. When this happens, the company is a lesser place.

To ensure that I encouraged contrary thinking and open communications, I developed a number of philosophies:

- I believed that the conflict that arose out of contrary thinking was just energy and simply needed to be managed.
- I definitely wanted different points of view from my staff. If we were all thinking alike, then some of us were redundant.
- I would not surround myself with yes women or yes men. My first senior food and beverage person at MLSE liked almost all my ideas. But my expertise was not food and beverages, so I knew there was no way that all my ideas were good. He had to go, in favour of someone who was much more confident, and could educate me and the organization about that side of the business.
- Not all decisions have to be supported unanimously. Sometimes the contrary thinker wins out.
- Once the contrary thinking is fully listened to and the debate is over, then the entire team is expected to follow the Seattle Seahawks' axiom, "We don't all have to be the same, but we have to play as one."
- And finally, you do not shoot the messenger if you ever hope to encourage contrary thinking on your team.

It's important to remember that if a leader's or a company's thinking is closed off to contrary thinking, and they behave like they have all the answers, then they are living in a dangerous bubble. In 1972, psychologist Irving Janis came up with the term "groupthink." This phenomenon occurs when "a group makes faulty decisions because group pressures lead to a deterioration of 'mental efficiency, reality testing and moral judgement.'"

Your leadership position and success are vulnerable if you shut yourself off from outside opinions. Great leaders embrace contrary thinkers.

LESSON 6

21 TIPS FROM PROVEN LEADERS

AT THE LATER STAGES OF MY CAREER, I think I had an excellent grasp of what it takes to be a great leader. I became a lifelong student of leadership, and I've shared much of what I learned with you in this book. To round out and complement my own perspective, I have also reached out to twenty-one other leaders whom I admire and asked each of them to share one leadership tip with you. I have found their insights invaluable over the years and I hope you'll also find something useful to take away from their words of wisdom.

I purposely picked leaders with different backgrounds and from different walks of life. Included are leaders from the community, business, and, of course, from the sports world. Ten of them are women and eleven are men, to reflect a gender balance as well.

I did not give these contributors any direction on what content they should submit. However, I must admit that I was pleased to see that many of them reinforced much of the same advice that I, myself, have given elsewhere in the book. Some of them worried that their tip would be similar to what others had submitted and volunteered to change what they had written if that was the case. I said not to worry, as I believe that a little redundancy reinforces that the tip must be a very important one.

• • • • •

1: PAUL GODFREY

President & CEO, Post Media Network

A leader and city builder who has worn more diverse leadership hats than anyone I have known (politics, media, baseball, real estate) and a trusted friend and advisor to so many.

PAUL: ***"Senior leadership falls into the hands of a very few people."***

" Ask any true leader what comes first, confidence or success, and the answer will always be confidence! The rank and file will follow the individual who exudes confidence without arrogance, and whose leadership approach demonstrates decisiveness. The philosophy of true leadership is, 'It's always better to be blamed for the things you do rather than the things you don't do.' "

2: DR. DANA SINCLAIR

Psychologist, Human Performance International

I got to know Dana when she was the psychologist for both the Leafs and Raptors. She was immensely helpful to our teams at MLSE, and today she helps a gold-medal list of sports clients: Detroit Lions, Los Angeles Dodgers, Portland Trail Blazers, Arizona Diamondbacks, Anaheim Ducks, and Calgary Flames. Dana helps those teams make the right draft choices and assists their young players with their journey through the pros.

DANA: ***"Avoiding the Red Flag"***

" 'Red Flag' is the category to which I assign those players/employees who will consistently fail to control their emotions under pressure, both on and off the field. Due to their talent, this lack of self-regulation is often rationalized and tolerated by management. A player or leader who is toxic in terms of low impulse control, a lack of self-discipline, questionable conscious restraint, or an unwillingness to see others' points of view can easily destroy the organization's culture of performance, which took years to develop. As past behaviour is the best predictor of future behaviour, don't be fooled by the 'Red Flag's' periodic bouts of good behaviour; these individuals are rarely able to change. ”

3: JOHN CASSADAY

Former President & CEO, Corus Entertainment

Like I did at MLSE, John has also used his consumer products background, at General Foods and Campbell Soup in his case, to help him have a tremendously successful career in broadcast at CTV and Corus. Of all the leaders mentioned in this book, John's leadership style is most similar to mine. It will be interesting to see what John's next challenge will be, as he still has a great deal to offer in his next senior leadership position. I was hoping it was going to be president and CEO of MLSE but that did not work out—he would have been a great leader for the company and its people.

JOHN: ***"Hire tough, manage easy."***

“ Not sure where I picked this leadership lesson up, but I believe they are words to live by. Katie Taylor, former CEO of the Four Seasons Hotel chain, once told me that not a maintenance worker, a doorman, or a dishwasher gets hired without at least four interviews. So for me, I advise managers to hire for values above competence, and get a lot of input; then you can manage easy. We've all made mistakes in hiring and then we spend time managing tough—trying to make our hiring mistake seem like their failure.

This is what one should look for when hiring:
1. alignment with your values
2. ambition, or a burning desire to succeed
3. integrity, which is the governor of unbridled ambition
4. and then . . . skills. ”

4: JENNIFER KEESMAAT

Chief City Planner, City of Toronto

Toronto Life magazine recognizes this "rock star" planner as the ninth most influential person in Toronto, and she has an excellent international reputation; the city is lucky to have her. If she had her way, Toronto would be both more functional and more liveable.

JENNIFER: ***"Leaders, by definition, are out in front, charting a new course, guided by principles and big ideas."***

“ As they say, it's lonely at the top. For this reason, it is critical to surround yourself with people who believe in your vision, who believe in your mandate, and who want to be part of the great change that you are facilitating. When you get knocked down, you are going to need people around you who can pick you up off the floor, dust you off, and push you back out to the front lines. Because that's what leaders do—they get back up again and again. Leaders know it's not easy; they don't expect change to result from just a little bit of effort. For this reason, leaders are persistent and tenacious. But to succeed, they also must be preoccupied with building a great team. ”

5: DALLAS EAKINS

Head Coach, San Diego Gulls, AHL

A complete coach who did an excellent job with the Marlies, developing young Leaf prospects. When he was hired by the Edmonton Oilers as their head coach, he was viewed as one of the hottest young coaches available. His first NHL head coaching gig did not work out so well, but he is a student of leadership and he will learn from the Edmonton experience. Dallas was on one of the MIT Sloan Sports Analytics panels in 2015. I asked him why he was interested in it, and he said it was "great to sit in on other sports—opens up my mind." Dallas Eakins—look for him behind another NHL bench soon.

DALLAS: ***"You had better be living what you are leading."***

"If you are going to be able to have the ability to affect and influence others to their benefit, you must be diligent every day to live the vision, live the process, and live the discipline.

"You can never waver, as everyone is watching your habits, focus, and your investment in time. You set the tone and your example is critical to your staff's success. Do not spend time with your staff; invest time with them. Every conversation, no matter the length or content, is an investment. Never pass up a time to invest your time in your people."

6: ROBIN BRUDNER

Former EVP, General Counsel, Maple Leaf Sports & Entertainment

One of my most trusted advisors at MLSE. I could always count on her intelligence, integrity, and ability to "lean in."

ROBIN: ***"A person's integrity permeates every message, every action, and every interaction."***

"It speaks to how you behave when people are watching and even when they are not. Integrity means being trustworthy, authentic, respectful, and empathetic. It requires courage to provide your true perspective, even if it may be unpopular, contrary to the majority view, or simply not what a person was hoping to hear. If you unwaveringly behave in a manner that exudes integrity, people will seek your leadership, want to join your team, and they will commit their best efforts to the betterment of the organization. Your reputation precedes, accompanies, and survives you. Having integrity will ensure yours is well respected and remembered. ”

7: DWANE CASEY

Head Coach, Toronto Raptors

He interviewed for the Raptors head coaching job in 2003, but did not get it. At the time I sent him a handwritten note, which he still has to this day, telling him that one day be would be a successful NBA head coach. He hasn't proven me wrong. When I told Dwane that I was using a leadership gym bag analogy in my book he said, "I try to reach into that leadership gym bag all the time."

DWANE: ***"Leadership is as important in sports as it is in any area of an organization."***

“ As a leader, the more you expect, the more you will get. If you expect a perfect game, you will never get one; but you are always pushing the team to get there. When I first got to Toronto, I wanted to change the perception of the Raptors being a soft, non-defensive team. We had to change that perception and establish a culture of toughness and an expectation defensively that would help us be a playoff team.

“As a leader, one of the main things I must do is to forge a set of principles, goals, and roles that are non-negotiable. I am a firm believer in having the players as part of the process, where we can share the same goals. This will allow them to have ownership in the process. Leaders cannot get caught up in the wrong things, like the power of notoriety. The things that have nothing to do with winning will help you fail.

“Lastly, one of the most important things a leader must do is to be totally prepared. There will not be a coach or player more prepared for an upcoming opponent than me. That in itself will set the tone of excellence. It's about having a consistent approach daily. Building a championship program in the NBA is a long, hard process. Key to all of this is excellent leadership.”

8: PATTI-ANNE TARLTON

COO, Ticketmaster Canada

Before her present role with Ticketmaster, as one of my excellent vice presidents at MLSE she put the "entertainment" in Maple Leaf Sports & Entertainment by making Air Canada Centre one of the top five music venues in the world.

PATTI-ANNE: ***"Be personable, yet don't take business personally."***

> "Get good at something that adds value, and network. Build and tirelessly represent your lifelong network. Travel solo, as this will push you to broaden your perspective. Seek out collaboration opportunities. It is not enough to personally succeed—others must too. Continually connect the dots between people, projects, and business. Project optimism. Your ability to recover from setbacks and remain positive will leave your mind open for creativity. Strive for an equal balance between big dreams, accomplishments, and having fun. Build your network around this principle."

9: RAHUL BHARDWAJ

President & CEO, Toronto Foundation

Toronto Life magazine recognizes him as the thirty-first most influential person in the city. A city builder who definitely adds bricks to the civic foundation and, I believe, a possible future mayor. Rahul leads a foundation that manages more than $411 million dollars and channels the money into neighbourhoods in need. Their mission and vision is to connect philanthropy to community needs and opportunities—to make Toronto the best place to live, work, learn, and grow through the power of giving. I am very proud to be on their board of directors.

RAHUL: ***"The key to leadership is knowing what to do with it."***

"It is critically important to have a long-term vision and then to develop the right culture and values to drive towards achieving that vision. In my experience, I've seen many people confuse managing with leading, getting lost in the day-to-day minutiae while losing sight of the long-term vision. It is not possible to lead effectively without vision, and that begins with answering the question, 'What are we doing this for?' and then constantly evaluating choices and decisions against that answer."

10: CHANTAL VALLÉE

Head Coach, University of Windsor Lancers Women's Basketball Team

She took over a historically losing program and turned it into a Canadian women's basketball dynasty, winning five consecutive Canadian intercollegiate championships. Defending CIS's Bronze Baby award was a very difficult task in 2015. Two Lancer all-stars and clear team leaders had graduated and were playing professional basketball in Europe. Two other players, including one of her important bigs, got injured and could not play. Chantal has been one heck of a coach during her entire championship run; but her coaching during the 2014-15 season was probably her most impressive. Five years ago, I promised her that I would buy the team rings if they won a national championship. That promise has turned out to be a very expensive one for me.

CHANTAL: ***"The principle of 'truth vs. harmony'"***

"When I started coaching I was under the misconception that creating a harmonious team was the key to being successful. Instead I needed to be clear, not harmonious.

"It is important that a coach not mislead players with broken promises, glorified role descriptions, or confusing expectations. My failure to be clear and tell the 'truth' usually resulted from fear of offending or losing harmony, and this became the very reason for team dysfunction. Disappointed and confused players were quick to point to my faults, inherently creating a disharmonious team.

"By providing clear expectations, the onus of team harmony is now placed on the players. Each can now accept or reject their role and the opportunity placed before them. With this understanding I am now able to firmly hold the team reins, and call them on it if needed. I have found that choosing truth over harmony has had the biggest impact in leading my teams to championship success."

11: CHRIS OVERHOLT

CEO, Canadian Olympic Committee

When you read Chris's tip, you will understand why he is one of the most respected and trusted leaders in sports and business. His twenty-year résumé reads like a fantasy check list for anyone who has ever dreamed of working in the sports business: MLSE, Florida Panthers, Miami Dolphins, and now leading the Canadian Olympic Committee. In his time at COC he has helped lead the organization to unprecedented growth on the business side, while helping Canada's elite athletes reach new levels of excellence.

CHRIS: ***"Business is personal. And we like it that way, don't we?"***

"The fact is that people enjoy doing business with those they genuinely like and respect. It makes everything easier, don't you think? The more difficult conversations are somehow more easily overcome, the exchange more genuine and relaxed. Honesty pervades. When we take a personal approach to our business, the engagements are more rewarding, and the challenges are somehow more fun. When these conditions exist, the barriers start to fall away and the air is primed for creativity, frankness, and results-focused outcomes. There is no pretence and it becomes easier to find compromise when needed because both parties want the other to succeed.

"It is often the case when we are young that we don't truly appreciate the importance of our personal and professional relationships. Perhaps at times we treat them casually, maybe on occasion even carelessly. But strong personal connections and genuine relationships inside and outside of business are the currency of a fruitful, happy life and career. Help enough people get what they might like, and you will almost always be rewarded for your support and caring. It is a basic life principle that is difficult to deny. So go ahead—phone a friend and get to work. ”

12: ROSEMARIE McCLEAN

SVP and COO, Ontario Teachers' Pension Plan

Her role is an important one for this $154 billion pension fund. OTPP was created by Claude Lamoureux and Bob Bertram twenty-five years ago and over that time has delivered an average return of ten percent per year, at the minuscule expense cost of 0.28 percent. The fund's 129,000 retired teachers are incredibly well served. Rosemarie is responsible for key activities like information technology, project management, and the financial operations that support their millions of dollars of investments. I knew Rosemarie the entire time I worked for MLSE, and I was delighted to see her rise through the ranks. Her quote below is very consistent with some of the other lessons in this book. And I want to stress again that, despite what many people think, Teachers' never turned down a general manager's request for money to sign or trade for a player at MLSE. Never!

ROSEMARIE: ***"Leaders need to realize they are being watched."***

“ Modern leaders must deal with a complex web of relationships. People choose to follow leaders who demonstrate integrity, compassion, and a bias for developing others. And how do people assess their leaders? They base it largely on observation. That means that you are being watched—a lot. So your actions need to be consistent with your words. Employees have told me that a small thing such as using their name when greeting them in the hallway makes a difference. It is daily behaviour, not the rally speech, that has the biggest impact. ”

13: PAUL ALOFS

President & CEO, The Princess Margaret Cancer Foundation

I introduce Paul more completely in Lesson 10. He has successfully learned his leadership expertise from the numerous industries and companies he has worked in. They say that one can learn much from teaching; Paul has learned even more from writing his bestselling book, *Passion Capital.*

PAUL: ***"Seize your moment—seize your passion."***

“ In the movie *Boyhood*, there is dialogue between two characters that goes like this: 'You know how everyone's always saying seize the moment? I don't know. I'm kind of thinking it's the other way around, you know, like the moment seizes us.' This was a stunning insight for me. I would apply this insight to passion. In my view, it's about seizing your passion. I am sure that you need to seize your passion as opposed to waiting for your passion to seize you. You need to start writing a plan with a creed or a powerful statement of what you believe in. Your creed is your promise to the world. You need to know how to take hold of your passion and to put it to work as your most valuable asset. ”

14: JUSTINE FEDAK

SVP and Head of Brand, Advertising and Sponsorships, BMO Financial Group, North America

I met Justine when we were negotiating the BMO stadium title deal and the bank's name on the TFC jersey kit. Justine is a great corporate partner and one of the most energetic, can-do, optimistic people I know. She has such a powerful presence, I started calling her the "Bank Lady." She liked this so much she now has a car license plate that reads, "BNKLY." I forgive her for becoming a Chicago Bulls fan.

JUSTINE: ***"Being a leader is having the guts to take risks and admit that you don't have all the answers."***

“ It's about listening to what is said, and what's not being said. Empowering teams is about putting them forward to make decisions, and for them to try things on their own. Leading is getting people to open up and openly challenge you. If they ask you for advice and then openly discuss their own successes or failures with you, then you are succeeding as a leader. ”

15: BRIAN BURKE

President of Hockey Operations, Calgary Flames

A proven winner with numerous NHL franchises and a Stanley Cup winner in Anaheim. Outspoken, opinionated, tough, smart, and one of the best standup friends I have ever had. I love how quickly he has turned around the Calgary Flames.

BRIAN: ***"Great leadership is a combination of brains and balls."***

> "One has to be decisive, and smarter than most of the group. He or she has to want to carry the burden of leadership and be comfortable with the loneliness that often comes with it. They also have to be able to listen well and be flexible."

16: VAL ACKERMAN

Commissioner, Big East Conference

Val was an Academic All-America basketball player at the University of Virginia and received a law degree from UCLA. She was the founding president of the Women's National Basketball Association (WNBA) and served as its president from 1996 until 2005. A twenty-six-year career in business and sports (including years as a special assistant to former NBA commissioner, David Stern) has given her the perspective on leadership she shares here.

VAL: ***"Not everyone will go on to become the leader of the free world."***

"But there's still plenty of room in our society for capable, energetic people who are very good at what they do, can make smart decisions, and don't panic when confronted with difficult tasks. If you think the world is full of problems, find a way to be a problem-solver and you will have permanent employment. Don't be afraid to look critically at situations and think to yourself, would a new approach work here? How can this be made better?

"In my experience, there's room in most any field for big thinking and fresh ideas, so never shy away from using your imagination and embracing a spirit of curiosity in whatever it is you decide to do."

17: MARK ABBOTT

President and Deputy Commissioner,
Major League Soccer

As MLS's very first employee back in 1993, he was hugely instrumental in keeping the league afloat in the early days, and helping its robust growth to twenty-two teams in the last few years. Mark apologized to me for being slow sending me this quote. He had a pretty valid reason: He was in labour negotiations with the MLS Players Union that could have delayed the start of the 2015 season. I imagine he actually used his own tip to help negotiate a successful labour agreement. I am happy that he got a new CBA done so the MLS season could start on time.

MARK: ***"Energy and Engagement"***

"You need to engage with those who don't agree with you more often and more intensely than with those that do. You need to continue to search for solutions when you are convinced that all alternatives have been considered. Be sure to seek counsel from others even if you (mistakenly) believe you don't need it. And be sure to engage when it is the last thing you want to do, but the first thing that someone else needs."

18: MARNIE McBEAN

Olympic Gold Medallist, bestselling author, and inspirational speaker

Marnie proudly represented Canada in rowing for many years, and won three gold medals and one silver in the 1992 and 1996 Olympics. Today Marnie is a champion of the Canadian Olympic movement and actively contributes to education about, and the advancement of issues around, sexual identification.

MARNIE: ***"Do you listen, or . . . do you wait to talk?"***

"How often do you find yourself waiting for the person responding to a question to breathe so that you can insert the answer that you already have in your head? We learn nothing when we are convinced that we know the answer before we've heard it. Having an answer is responsible, even expected from every leader; but knowing all the answers is unlikely. Be curious as to how others would solve a problem. If you ask a question or someone offers their perspective, listen to what they have to say; then weigh it out. This will show that you value the person that you are talking to and you might just learn how to take a forward leap that's been eluding you. ”

19: HARRY ROSEN

Founder and Executive Chairman, Harry Rosen Inc.

As a youth he learned about making men's clothes and, equally importantly, about men's buying habits. After dropping out of high school, he opened Harry Rosen Inc. with his brother Lou. Today Harry Rosen's sixteen stores offer the gold standard in Canadian luxury menswear and his name has become an iconic brand. Even today one can still see Harry "walking the talk" in his stores.

HARRY: ***"As the founder of Harry Rosen's, I have provided the vision and shared that with all my colleagues over all the years."***

“ As a leader, I have found it invaluable to frequently work the selling floor in my stores. By interacting with our customers, I am able to learn how our merchandise offerings are being received and gain valuable insights into the quality of service we provide. This dedication to our vision, quality, and service has resulted in successful growth, a leading share of the better menswear business, and created strong brand identity. ”

20: TANYA TODOROVIC

Partner, Odgers Berndtson

I first met Tanya at the 2015 Georgie-Odette Leadership Symposium at the University of Windsor, where she was one of fourteen speakers on leadership. Prior to joining the search firm Odgers Berndtson as a partner specializing in the growing non-profit sector, she had human resource roles in both the private and public sector. At the symposium, Tanya called on her professional search perspective to give the audience unique insight into what important things interviewers are looking for in a leadership candidate.

TANYA: ***"Passion and enthusiasm are key differentiators between leaders."***

“ As part of my job as a headhunter, I have had the good fortune of interviewing hundreds of senior executives over many years. I have seen that an individual's level of interest in an opportunity has direct impact on whether they are selected as the successful candidate. Without passion and a deep interest in the mandate of the organization, experience has shown that the likelihood of a leader exiting when the going gets tough is high. Without passion and enthusiasm, leaders will also not be able to effectively motivate their team. Those making the hiring decision know this and look for evidence of it in the interview discussions. In the final stages of selection, this passion and enthusiasm are key differentiators between candidates. ”

21: DR. BRUCE KIDD

Former Warden of Hart House; VP, University of Toronto; and Principal, University of Toronto Scarborough

An academic, author, and Olympian, Bruce was my first choice to head up the MLSE Foundation because his thinking ran contrary to the rest of the senior leadership team at MLSE, and because he had a long track record of passionately giving back to the community. A proud "socialist," Bruce was the one who introduced me to the thought of supporting Olivia Chow for mayor of Toronto.

BRUCE: ***"Consult as much as possible."***

“ Given the complexity of the decisions we make, and the many stakeholders those decisions affect, it always helps to get others' views on an issue and potential courses of action. It takes nothing away from your authority to consult; on the contrary, it strengthens

> your position as an engaged leader and it really helps with your peripheral vision. Invariably it leads to better ideas. But don't consult forever—that can lead to indecision and demobilization. Have a clear cycle of consultation, then decide, communicate your decision, and then implement. ”

• • • • •

To create this important chapter, Lesson 6, I gave a lot of thought to whom I would ask to contribute, and I feel that I have succeeded in gathering a powerful group of proven leaders from the three areas of business, sports, and the community. I am especially pleased that almost everyone I asked to contribute agreed to do so. A big thanks to all of my friends for taking the time. I might also add that if you ever get a chance to work with, or for, any of these individuals, you will be a better leader for the experience.

LESSON 7

BEST PRACTICES: LEGITIMATE PLAGIARISM

I DON'T THINK I HEARD THE ACTUAL TERM "best practices" until around the mid-nineties, even though, as it turned out, I had been practicing the concept much earlier than that at both Hostess Foods and Pillsbury. During those first two stints as a company president, I clearly understood that one could not steal another company's patent or plagiarize a song for a television ad. However, I also started to realize that there were a lot of great ideas from many diverse sources that could be adapted successfully for my own company's use.

I first learned of the term "legitimate plagiarism" when I read Robert Slater's book, *Jack Welch and the GE Way*. As I understood Welch's philosophy, it is not okay to plagiarize books, ignore patents, or steal formulas, but it is smart business to seek out public domain best practices, adapt them, and continually improve them. I willingly took the concept and applied it as a best practice in my own management style. Soon, my corporate career was full of legitimate plagiarism, and it pushed me and the companies I led to innovate and improve.

At Hostess we studied what Frito Lay was doing in their U.S. markets and often copied them in Canada before they could even bring their own new ideas into our market. At Pillsbury, the U.S. company introduced a preferred supplier grocery trade strategy that we adapted in Canada and made much better than theirs.

At MLSE we studied ESPN's sports bars. While we thought they had a good concept, we also thought it was being badly executed. We launched the Real Sports Bar & Grill with a better restaurant design, better audio-visual technology, and much better quality food. Within a year RSB&G was the highest grossing restaurant in Canada and was chosen as the best sports bar in North America. I visited the impressive L.A. Live entertainment centre in Los Angeles and realized that the video board in Maple Leaf Square needed to be much larger than we had originally planned.

I attended a Blue Jays game at Rogers Centre and purposely looked for best practices in game ops and stadium operations. It took me until the end of the ninth inning to find one. At the end of the game, the Blue Jays invited all the kids to come out and run the bases. The next week we had kids on the court after the Raptors game, shooting free throws.

With TFC, we heavily borrowed ideas from European football and created some of our own North American best practices that Seattle, Portland, and other MLS expansion franchises successfully adopted. Unfortunately, after a while I believe TFC then rested on its laurels, and the U.S. clubs passed us by with a lot of new fan initiatives of their own.

When we were planning for Air Canada Centre we turned the tables and actually did a worst practices analysis of how the orginal SkyDome designed and operated their premium suites. On a whiteboard we wrote down every one of their worst practices and then brainstormed how we could do those things better.

Being in three different professional sports leagues was also a boon for finding best practices to adopt at MLSE. The NBA leads the way with their Team Business Operations group, which gathers the best practices from all thirty clubs, shares them with the entire league, and then encourages all the clubs to use them. Actually they often did more than encourage them.

If then Commissioner David Stern really thought you were ignoring some good ideas, he would be sure to mention them in his usual forceful manner.

Adopting best practices, or legitimate plagiarism, is an excellent way to help you succeed in whatever field you are in. Beyond the corporate setting, best practices can also be very effective in the not-for-profit sector and in government. For example, if I were the mayor of Toronto, I would create a department of best practices so that every decision council made had the best learning from cities all over the world. Here are some thoughts to help you get comfortable with the acceptability of the concept, no matter what kind of organization you lead or work in:

“Don’t think that using best practices means you are not creative.”

- First of all, adapting ideas that are in the public domain is legal; it’s not plagiarism or stealing.
- Don’t think that using best practices means you are not creative. Very, very few of us are Steve Jobs. You can be creative making someone else’s best practice even better.
- You will find that some of your staff are either uncomfortable with the concept, or too lazy to do their best practices research. You need to make sure all your staff get over their hesitation. At MLSE, when any presentation was made to senior management, we paid close attention to whether the individual had done their best practices homework.
- Go and talk to companies and individuals from non-competing industries. Many of them will be happy to share their best practices with you.

Over most of my career, I constantly looked for best practices and ideas. I looked for them when I was out shopping. When I was running. I had a wide open mind when I listened to music, watched television, or went to art galleries. I found that ideas were all around me if I was just willing to look. Years ago I heard Edward de Bono talk about lateral thinking, so I began looking for best practices with his philosophy in mind. Today, the good leaders and good companies all study and adapt best practices.

LESSON 8

GOOD LEADERSHIP NEEDS SOME EDGE

IN LESSON 10, I RECOMMEND TWENTY-ONE BOOKS for you to read, including *The Leadership Engine: How Winning Companies Build Leaders at Every Level*, by Noel Tichy. I chose this book because it resonated with me in so many ways. I very much agree with what Tichy wrote about values, ideas, energy, and having a teachable point of view, because I have had good leadership experiences with all of these concepts.

When Tichy also talked about the need for leaders to have "edge—the courage to see reality and act upon it," that really struck home with me. Upon reflection I realized that I had always had a form of edge, in my ability to make tough decisions, to take action, and to have difficult conversations. I called on my edge to push MLSE to acquire a football team and to become a television broadcaster, even when support from my management team was often weak or almost non-existent. I pushed my vice presidents to let weak performers go. And I forcefully stood up for my ideas with my board of directors.

Even as a young leader I was quick to speak my mind and intercede when I saw things that I did not agree with. In fact I was probably fortunate that I did not get into trouble for being too outspoken. As a young leader, your edge will have to be under control, but it should increase as you gain more experience and confidence. It is not something that you can use a lot early in your career, but to be successful you will have to develop it in time.

"Edge is not something that you can use a lot early in your career, but to be successful you will have to develop it in time."

As I became more experienced and became more senior in companies, I became confident being more candid and decisive. Using edge to make business decisions was seldom tough for me to do. I found implementing a new business strategy or discontinuing an old, under-performing one was quite easy. However, using edge to make people decisions was always damn tough.

• • • • •

Tichy convinced me, in theory, that if I was going to be a better leader I needed to have more edge and have the ability to make people decisions in a timely way. That I had to have the courage of my convictions and the candour necessary to convey those convictions. At the same time, a Caliper Test (a personal assessment tool that discerns strengths, motivators, and the potential of an individual to succeed) reinforced my belief in the need to have some edge by showing me that senior leaders scored lower on empathy. There are times when a leader needs to be empathetic, but if the individual is consistently making excuses and dragging down the company as a result of his or her inaction, then he or she has to go. And finally, I embraced Jack Welch's edgy philosophy: "cruel and Darwinian—try fair and effective," on the need to differentiate (via bonuses, salaries, promotions, terminations) between poor, good, and very good employees.

In January 2014, Jack Zenger and Joseph Folkman published a study in the *Harvard Business Review* that even made a case for directing a bit of candour and edge at employees as well; it was entitled, "Your Employees Want the Negative Feedback You Hate to Give." In a study with a significant sample size of 899 people, they found that bosses hated giving negative feedback, but the data revealed the paradox that people believe constructive criticism is essential to their career development. "They want it from their leaders. But their leaders often don't feel comfortable offering it up."

From that they concluded that the ability to give corrective feedback is critical to effective leadership. Rather than avoiding offering constructive criticism to your employees, you should embrace the opportunity to coach them. This honest feedback can actually help to boost your team's performance, and set the organization apart overall.

Based on all this information and research, I really started pushing my managers and vice presidents at MLSE to lead with more edge and candour. To see how the philosophy was taking hold, every April I speed-read the hundreds of written employee evaluations that were completed. My reviews concluded that as an organization we were getting more comfortable with the concept of edge, but that we still had a long, long way to go.

"The ability to give corrective feedback is critical to effective leadership."

I will let Paulo Coelho, Brazilian lyricist and author of twenty-five books, have the last word on the ability to make tough decisions and deliver difficult messages: "Truth whether it is good or bad, it is liberating."

LESSON 9

ALWAYS TELL THE WHOLE STORY

MY FIRST REALLY SIGNIFICANT PROMOTION was to vice president at General Foods (whose brands include Kool-Aid, Jell-O, and Maxwell House coffee). Today you would know the company as Kraft Foods and once the Heinz-GF merger is complete I don't know what the company is going to be called. One day early in my new role, my boss came to talk to me about the quality of my monthly business postings. At the time, I was leading the cereals and cold beverage division and was expected to issue a monthly report on our progress, or lack thereof. My boss gave me a piece of communications advice that turned out to be much more helpful than just writing better monthly postings.

He told me that my communications had to tell a complete, but compact story. That I had to give context, provide rationale, and draw conclusions—all in as concise a format as possible. I followed his advice for the rest of my career. (Ironically, he also told me that I did not need to take public speaking lessons; but, given that he was such a lousy speaker, I ignored him and took them just the same.)

> **"Give context, provide rationale, and draw conclusions—all in as concise a format as possible."**

In her book, *Tough Truths*, Deirdre Maloney stresses that excellent communication is important because, "Top leaders know that every interaction is a chance to connect in an effective professional manner. Every time they speak or write, they do it with care, sending a clear message." From my observations and experience, Maloney is correct.

So many times I have seen leaders give a talk and it's clear that they gave it no thought in advance, were ill prepared, and were making up their remarks as they went along. Early in my career, I heard a lot of speakers start off their speeches with the joke, "I feel like Zsa Zsa Gabor's ninth husband. I know what to do, but I don't know how to make it interesting." I am sure I wasn't alone in the audience when I thought that if this speaker could not invest time to make their message interesting, then maybe they should have passed on giving the speech in the first place.

To this day I prepare notes ahead of time for every conference call and meeting. For speeches, I average about an hour of preparation (research, writing, rewriting, practice) for every minute I speak. I know I may not ever be the very best speaker, but I know I will always tell the whole story. My advice, always prepare when you know you will have to speak. Your employees, and anyone else you speak to, will notice that you gave real thought to your message.

• • • • •

Somewhere along the line, I either came up with the quote, or heard someone say, "Eighty percent of problems are caused by poor communications. But thankfully, eighty percent of the problems can be cured with great communications." Now, I can't vouch for the accuracy of the percentages, but directionally I believe that this formula is correct.

As a leader, I believed that my staff always wanted to know where the company was going. The rationale for why it was going in a certain direction. How we were progressing, or even if we were not progressing. And I knew to always include specific recognition for those who were positively contributing to the solutions. Criticism for those not contributing was always done in private. I never screamed. I never swore. If a department or an individual was screwing up, then we took it off to the side. I have absolutely no time for screaming bullies who believe that motivating by fear is effective. My strong belief is that being admired gives you much more leadership power than being feared.

One of the oldest beliefs in marketing is the "seven rule," which states that customers need to hear or see a message at least seven times before they will buy from you. Again, I don't know if seven, a number lower or higher than seven, is correct; but I do know that there has to be significant frequency and some redundancy in your messaging for you to be effective. And your message also has to be consistent.

At MLSE we communicated in so many ways: emails, voice mails, our intranet website, during training sessions, monthly recognition meetings, and, of course, one on one. The highlight of every year was our annual Town Hall meeting. This meeting was a major communications and recognition event and a huge "spectacle," held in the lower bowl of the Air Canada Centre arena. We had our in-house band, Play to Win, kick things off; usually an outside speaker; numerous business updates; and a terrific awards ceremony. It was an incredible opportunity to communicate with all our employees in a very high-impact way every year.

> **"A leader should make sure there is over-communication instead of risking that employees are not getting enough information."**

MLSE was a private company and our financial results were supposed to be confidential, so I started off all the meetings by telling my staff this: "As you know, we are a private company, but today we are going to share with you some very confidential information. And we are going to trust that you are professional and will know to do the right things with this information." Over the years, and despite incredible media scrutiny, I was disappointed only once, when a person (who had been fired after the Town Hall meeting) leaked out material information to the *Toronto Star*. I wasn't that upset with the fact that the *Star* ran the story. They had it and that's what newspapers do. However, what I do have trouble with is when the media runs a story quoting a couple of anonymous employees about alleged problems or issues in a company. Even great companies will always have a few disgruntled employees. It's easy to find "dirt" if you will listen to anyone and not drill down to get the real facts.

Over my years as a president, I am sure there were times when some people got tired of hearing some company messaging over and over again; but I strongly believe that a leader should make sure there is over-communication instead of risking that employees are not getting enough information. And by all means when you do communicate, be sure to tell the whole story.

LESSON 10

21 OF MY FAVOURITE LEADERSHIP BOOKS

"Each book is a mind alive, a life revealed, a world awaiting exploration." –Dean Koontz, Innocence

I START THIS CHAPTER WITH A QUOTE FROM DEAN KOONTZ for two reasons. One, I believe it is true and, secondly, to demonstrate that one can pick up ideas from all kinds of books. Who would think that an idea from a bestselling mystery, horror, and science fiction author could find its way into a book on leadership? I have long been convinced that if you keep your mind open, you will find leadership ideas are everywhere, just waiting to be discovered and personalized.

When I was on my *Dream Job* book tour, I gave talks at many universities and colleges across Canada. In my presentations I often quoted from books that I had read during my career and that helped me come up with my own leadership voice. Many times after these sessions, students or young professionals would come up to me and ask me to give them a list of recommended books to read. So I thought that if some of my audiences were interested in what books they might read, then maybe you are, too. Here goes—you may be surprised by some of my recommendations for books on "leadership."

• • • • •

1: IN SEARCH OF EXCELLENCE: LESSONS FROM AMERICA'S BEST-RUN COMPANIES

Thomas J. Peters and Robert H. Waterman

In 1982, Peters and Waterman published arguably one of the best business books of all time: *In Search of Excellence.* The two authors studied forty-three of America's best companies and came up with nine principal findings. When it came out in the 1980s, just about every president and vice president I knew read the book and many started acting on Peters's and Waterman's findings. As a brand new, rookie president of Hostess Foods, I was very taken by the book, especially the "Hands on—Value Driven" chapter that encouraged leaders to figure out their corporate and personal value system and to decide on what their company stood for.

I never had time to put their principles into practice at Hostess, but I did have great success implementing "value driven" at Pillsbury, SkyDome, and finally MLSE. Today I give *In Search of Excellence* a lot of credit for introducing me to the merits and strengths of having a clear, powerful vision and rock-solid, authentic values. If I was to identify the two core beliefs that best describe my leadership approach, they definitely would have to be vision and values. The original edition is thirty-three years old now, but a recently updated version is still a very relevant read on leadership.

2: THE INTANGIBLES OF LEADERSHIP: THE 10 QUALITIES OF SUPERIOR EXECUTIVE PERFORMANCE

Richard A, Davis, Ph.D.

One day the lead board member from Teachers', Erol Uzumeri, suggested that I meet with Dr. Davis. I thought it was simply going to be a meeting with an interesting industrial/organizational psychologist to have a nice, casual discussion. Years later, I learned that he was actually assessing me for Teachers'. I guess I passed.

As it turned out, Richard and I really hit it off. We talked for about three hours (duh—that should have been a dead giveaway that I was being assessed) about my career progression, my leadership beliefs, and the strategies I followed to lead the six companies that I had been president of over my career.

Davis told me that he was writing a book, but I didn't give that much thought until later, when I learned that he had used me as an example in his chapter entitled, "Will." He chose me for that chapter because of my perseverance in pursuing my basketball dream. He ended the chapter with advice that I very much agree with: "Be accountable for your own luck. Will success to occur."

Today I recommend *The Intangibles of Leadership* more than any other book. It effectively outlines ten leadership qualities, including Wisdom, Will, Integrity, Presence, Fallibility, and five others. In addition to the rich content, I like that a reader can read the chapters in any order they like, or read only the chapters that they think can help them. I like to think I have followed the same thinking with the way I structured the lessons in this book.

3: THE LEADERSHIP ENGINE: HOW WINNING COMPANIES BUILD LEADERS AT EVERY LEVEL

Dr. Noel M. Tichy

In 2004, I created an annual leadership course at MLSE called Elite Training. Elite because only eight managers or directors with the potential to be vice presidents were invited to take the course each year. It ran from late September to April, comprising forty-five hours of class time, outside speakers like Harry Rosen and Paul Alofs, and four marked assignments, culminating with a graduation presentation from MLSE chairman, Larry Tanenbaum.

Over the years, forty-eight senior staff members graduated from the program. Today many of them are vice presidents and three run their own companies. Each year I chose a course text that I thought would reinforce my leadership message and for the first few years that book was *The Leadership Engine.* Tichy's key message is that a leader should embrace five key must-haves: "ideas, values, energy, edge, and a teachable point of view." This book was written in 1997, so some of his corporate examples are a little dated, but his leadership message is still bang on.

4: WINNING
Jack Welch

Jack Welch had a tremendously successful forty-year career at General Electric. Over that time, he not only dramatically helped build GE's market capitalization, but he also developed hundreds of great future leaders.

There are a number of Jack Welch books, such as *Jack: Straight From the Gut, Jack Welch and the GE Way* (about him, not by him), and this one that I am recommending to you. I read all of those Jack Welch books and learned something from each one, but the one takeaway that I liked best was in chapter three of *Winning*, entitled, "Cruel and Darwinian—Try Fair and

Effective." In this chapter he wrote about the importance of differentiating between the top and bottom performers in any business. It was not until I read this book that I discovered that the idea of creating a meritocracy at MLSE was the way to go. Interestingly, to be able to successfully differentiate, you need the edge that Tichy believes in.

5: AN ASTRONAUT'S GUIDE TO LIFE ON EARTH

Chris Hadfield

As you now know from Lesson 1, and you may know from my first book, *Dream Job*, I strongly believe in the power of having a corporate or personal dream. You also know from Lesson 3 that I really champion the need to "get your ticket punched" if you ever hope to realize your dream. Hadfield's book clearly supports both ideas.

Until I read this book, I thought that writing down my dream to run an NBA team and spending twenty-nine years preparing to realize that role was pretty special. Well, that was until I read Hadfield's book. He first dreamed of being an astronaut when he was only nine, and when there were zero Canadian astronauts. I thought that my working through years in consumer products, facility management, and broadcast was an impressive way to get my ticket punched. Again, Hadfield took getting one's ticket punched to a much higher level (forgive the pun). From getting his pilot's licence at an early age, to military training, becoming a fighter pilot, a test pilot, and even learning how to speak Russian, he did everything to realize his dream.

If you enjoyed looking at his breathtaking photographs and educational videos when he was orbiting the earth, and you are a young leader looking to be motivated to dream big, you will love this book.

6: LEAN IN: WOMEN, WORK AND THE WILL TO LEAD

Sheryl Sandberg

I like to think I earned a reputation for hiring, helping develop, and promoting strong women in the workforce. First at Pillsbury, then SkyDome, and finally at MLSE, I worked with a number of outstanding women. Three of them—Robin Brudner, Dana Sinclair, and Patti-Anne Tarlton—all give leadership tips in Lesson 6.

Unfortunately, in my career I sometimes witnessed unfair stereotyping, sexism, and even occasionally an anti-woman bias when it came to awarding roles, giving promotions, or paying fair compensation. As I became more experienced, and probably more enlightened, I like to think I dealt with those issues in the companies I led. However, it wasn't until Facebook COO Sandberg wrote *Lean In*, the blockbuster guide to female achievement, that I realized even more clearly that women really have a very difficult job being heard, and hence her belief that women need to speak up more—to be unafraid to be contrary and, if necessary, to "lean in."

When I finished reading Sandberg's book, I immediately sent an email to over twenty women whom I admire, and encouraged them to read it. I also sent it to a half-dozen men who

I thought would find her message important. Today I continue to encourage young women to read the book, hoping that they will learn to "lean in" too.

One item in the book that I really found appalling was the Harvard Business School "Heidi/Howard" case study. Hopefully you are like me, and you will also find the test results disappointing.

7: FIXING THE GAME: BUBBLES, CRASHES, AND WHAT CAPITALISM CAN LEARN FROM THE NFL

Dr. Roger L. Martin

I have long admired the Rotman School of Management program: the faculty, the facilities, their speaker series, and their former dean, Roger Martin. Roger is very well know for authoring eight books and many articles in the *Harvard Business Review*, among other publications.

When I picked up his book, *Fixing the Game*, I expected to read about the good and bad of capitalism, and I sure did. In fact, when I finished the book, I emailed Roger to say that I really enjoyed reading his book, but the complexity and breadth of his conclusions and solutions actually depressed me. Depressed me because the problems seem so large, and the appetite and enthusiasm for correcting them seem so small.

What I did not realize when I picked up the book was how much his thoughts on the evolution of the civil foundation, and how to fix it, would resonate with me. His concept that companies can have a negative, neutral, or positive impact on society made me think about some things differently, and even start to change the way I did things. The idea caused me to fight with my editor of *Dream Job* to include a chapter entitled, "On Building a City—One Dream, One Brick at a Time." To take on the role of co-chair of the Olivia Chow campaign for mayor of Toronto—surprising to many, including me. And, finally, to make sure that one of the lessons in this book addresses the need for leaders to "add bricks to the civil foundation." I hope that this book and Roger Martin's book will get you to think more about the community you lead and live in. And how you can make it a more liveable place for all.

8: DREAM BIG DREAMS: THE JACK DONOHUE STORY

Mike Hickey

I first met the late Jack Donohue when Larry Tanenbaum put together an advisory group to help bring an NBA expansion franchise to Toronto. Jack was on our bid team because he was synonymous with Canadian basketball, having headed up the national team for seventeen years. The expansion application was successful in Toronto getting a franchise; however, the Tanenbaum-Peddie team lost fair and square to the Slaight-Bitove team. After that, Jack and I lost touch for a bit, but when Slaight bought out Bitove and made me president of the Raptors, we actively resumed our friendship. It was a rare month that we didn't talk about basketball, the NBA, and, of course, the Raptors.

Jack was terrific. I always took his calls because he was a very nice guy and because he did so much for Canadian basketball. Today, people talk a lot about Vince Carter and the Raptors motivating Tristan Thompson, Andrew Wiggins, Anthony Bennett, and many other young Canadians to aspire to a future in the NBA; but Jack predated all of that. He helped the Canadian men's basketball team to dream big and ultimately exceed expectations in two Olympics. Personally, he had a very positive influence on me, enabling me to open up about my ambitions in *Dream Job*. When I turned sixty, to celebrate my birthday and in recognition of Jack, Colleen and I arranged for a maple tree to be planted on the Toronto waterfront with a plaque that reads, "Dream Big Dreams—Jack Donohue."

9: A YEAR OF LIVING GENEROUSLY: DISPATCHES FROM THE FRONT LINES OF PHILANTHROPY

Lawrence Scanlan

This may be another surprising book suggestion for you, but one that is very much in tune with my lesson on "Add Bricks to the Civil Foundation." It shows how one person got involved and gave back to various communities.

When I first came up with the idea of writing *Dream Job*, I hired Michael Levine as my agent. After reading my book prospectus, he told me that to have a successful book I needed professional help. So he introduced me to Larry Scanlan. Larry has had an impressive writing career as a journalist and is an established author with fourteen books to his credit.

Larry and I are quite different people, but we hit it off very well and our writing process worked smoothly. Over nine months, I wrote almost 90,000 words and passed them on to Larry. I like to say that Larry made me sound literate. I know that *Dream Job* would never have been published without Larry's help.

To get to know Larry, I read a couple of his books. One was called, *A Year of Living Generously: Dispatches from the Front Lines of Philanthropy*. Over the course of twelve months, Larry volunteered to work in twelve organizations, from a drop-in centre in Kingston, Ontario, to Habitat for Humanity, to one of Canada's most notorious prisons, Millhaven.

One day, I asked Larry what his main takeaway was from those twelve months on the front lines. He said, "I now have trouble saying no to people."

10: OUTLIERS: THE STORY OF SUCCESS

Malcolm Gladwell

I have long been a fan of most of Gladwell's books (including *Blink* and *David and Goliath*); but *The Tipping Point* and *Outliers* are easily my favourites. One year, in our MLSE strategic plan we discussed at length our fear of a possible Maple Leafs tipping point, due to the changing demographics of Toronto. One of our directors, and definitely one of Toronto's best corporate lawyers, Dale Lastman, really encouraged us to take action. Based on this fear, we increased our investment in marketing and community events, and advertised the Marlies as an affordable introduction into the Leafs' family. With Toronto's continued demographic changes, the rise of the Raptors, and the Leafs' lack of success on the ice, I suggest that the danger of a Leafs' tipping point is still pretty valid.

I also found *Outliers* an interesting read. Even though some of Gladwell's research examples have been challenged since the book was published, his material still got me thinking. "People at the very top don't just work harder, or even much harder than everyone else. They work much, much harder," was not a surprise to me at all, but unfortunately goes against many Millennials' strong desire for work-life balance. The ideas he covered in his two sections called "Opportunity" and "Legacy" got me thinking out of the box. *Outliers* is a challenging read and not for everyone, but I suggest you give it a shot.

11: GOOD TO GREAT: WHY SOME COMPANIES MAKE THE LEAP . . . AND OTHERS DON'T
Jim Collins

I like Collins's work because his books, like *Good to Great*, *Built to Last*, and *Great by Choice*, reinforce my belief in the importance and benefits of vision and values, while giving me some good ideas on how to use them successfully in the leadership of a company.

Early in this book, he introduces twelve business myths and how visionary companies addressed them. If you have any doubts about the merits of vision and values, I suspect they will largely be answered by that section alone. I also take comfort that despite the book being written back in 1994, the eighteen visionary companies he used as positive examples are mostly doing pretty well (including Walt Disney, GE, American Express, Boeing, Procter & Gamble, among others). The comparison companies, not so well. Still a very worthwhile read if you are a young (or not so young) leader.

12: PASSION CAPITAL: THE WORLD'S MOST VALUABLE ASSET

Dr. Paul Alofs

I will declare my bias right off the bat on this choice. Paul was born and grew up in Windsor. He graduated from the University of Windsor and, like me, has been awarded an honorary doctorate from Windsor as well as the Alumni Achievement Award. He also started his career at Colgate and then had his ticket punched at HMV, BMG Music, Disney Stores, and MP3.com. Today he is the very successful president and CEO of The Princess Margaret Cancer Foundation, which raises about $100 million a year for cancer research.

Paul is also very much a vision and values leader. His vision statement at Princess Margaret is a very clear and compelling one: "To conquer cancer in our lifetime." Paul is also a very passionate guy about what he believes in, and all that he does. I remember talking to him when I was retiring from MLSE and the search for my replacement was just starting. I thought Paul could be a great candidate and encouraged him to toss his hat in the ring. Paul said thanks but no thanks, because he was so committed to the hospital's vision and so loyal to all its supporters that he couldn't possibly leave the foundation until his work was done.

Paul's book, *Passion Capital*, is a great read because it so clearly articulates that to successfully realize one's dream requires a great deal of passion. That you need this intense desire and enthusiasm to be able to perform better and weather the inevitable storms during your career. As the cover of his book says, "Passion capital is a revolutionary asset that will completely change your idea of how to build long-term success for your career, company or cause." Passion capital—a good formula and a good read.

13: THE 7 HABITS OF HIGHLY EFFECTIVE PEOPLE: POWERFUL LESSONS IN PERSONAL CHANGE

Stephen Covey

Another leadership book standard. I read Covey's when I was starting at SkyDome—a brand new job and a brand new industry for me. I was completely overwhelmed, learning about a company that had only been in operation for a little over three months and was in complete organizational disarray. On top of that, I was an entirely green sports and entertainment rookie. My challenge was to get up to speed very quickly in order to be effective. This book helped me do that then, and over the years I have gone back and referenced it a great deal. Today, my copy is dog-eared and numerous sections are highlighted in yellow. I like that Covey is another big fan of vision and values. His Habit Number One encourages you to be proactive, and Habit Number Two says, "Begin with the end in mind."

14: LEADERSHIP

Rudolph Giuliani

DON'T BUY THIS BOOK! Okay—so why would I put it on my list of books if I did not want you to read it? Well, for a couple of reasons. I was attracted to this book because of its title (obviously) and the role Giuliani played as mayor of New York after the 9/11 terrorist attacks in 2001.

As you browse through bookstores or go online to figure out which books on leadership might be interesting to you, you will "kiss a lot of frogs." By that I mean that a book may look good on the shelf or on your iPad, but about fifty percent of the time the book will not be worth the price. That said, if you can pick up one piece of learning that sticks with you, then the book may just have been worth the price after all.

Overall I thought that the Giuliani book had little to offer in leadership wisdom, but the one thing that resonated with me was his chapter entitled, "Weddings Are Optional, but Funerals Are Mandatory." He made that point after attending many funerals for the New York first responders who died on that horrible day. That one point in a bad book really stuck with me.

A few years after I read *Leadership*, one of my favourite professors, Max Brownlie, died and attending the funeral in Windsor was going to be a real challenge for me, as my calendar in Toronto was jammed. But I remembered Giuliani's quote and knew immediately that I had to be there. When I walked into the memorial reception following the funeral, his family was very surprised and pleased that I had showed up to pay my respects to a great professor and a good man. Today, funerals continue to be mandatory for me.

And if my DON'T BUY THIS BOOK recommendation is not enough to scare you away from this author, Google his name and read about his repeatedly intolerant and racist behaviour over the past few years.

15: ACTUALLY, I RECOMMEND ANY OF THE THIRTY-NINE BOOKS WRITTEN BY AUTHOR, CONSULTANT, EDUCATOR, AND "THE FATHER OF MODERN MANAGEMENT," Peter Drucker

Wikipedia describes Drucker as an individual who "contributed to the philosophical and practical foundations of the modern business corporation." During my years in business school, I had my own mini-library of his books. *Managing for Results* was such an early book on business strategy that it was far ahead of its time; so far that Drucker chose not to put the word "strategy" in the title. In the 1960s, "strategy" was more of a military concept, not a business concept.

The Effective Executive: The Definitive Guide to Getting the Right Things Done delivered an important message to me as a young leader, specifically eight lessons on how to be more effective in school and in business. And *The Age of Discontinuity*, which outlined four areas of discontinuity (technology, world economy, mass education, a more pluralistic society), was quite prophetic and, frankly, way beyond my grasp at the time. If you want to go back to the roots of business thinking, Drucker is a great place to start.

16: HOW TO WIN FRIENDS AND INFLUENCE PEOPLE
Dale Carnegie

This book is a 1936 classic, so its message is much older than anyone who will ever read this book. One of the early self-help books, over 115,000,000 copies have been sold. Due to its continuing popularity, it was updated in 1981. Today you can go online and buy it for $0.99!

The reason I read the book was more out of curiosity than anything else. Back in the 1970s when I was at General Foods, I worked for a really horrible leader. I honestly believed this man took time on Friday afternoons to chew me out so that he could personally wreck my weekends. I was having a very bad time working for him and was actively considering leaving the company just to escape him. However, in a roundabout way, I found that the company president also disliked him, and was about to send him back to the parent company in the States. So I waited this bad boss out and, sure enough, he was soon sent packing; and I was promoted to vice president.

The day before he left, in a rare moment of civility, he invited me out for lunch to give me some parting advice. He was late for the lunch and explained that his tardiness was due to the fact that he was out looking for a book to give me: *How to Win Friends and Influence People*. When he told me this, I almost laughed out loud; here was a leader so lacking in self-awareness he had no idea what others thought about him, and he believed that *I* was the one who needed to read this book.

After he left and I took on my new senior role, my curiosity caused me to buy the book to understand just what he had hoped to tell me. While I do not think this bad boss taught me anything positive himself, his book recommendation turned out to be pretty good. Carnegie's book reinforced to me some valid and timeless beliefs. Things like: give honest and sincere appreciation, always remember a person's name, be a good listener, show respect for others, and many more. So, as it turns out, one can learn something even from a bad leader. It's also important that you prepare yourself for having the inevitable bad boss, maybe even a few of them over the course of your career.

17: ON BECOMING A LEADER
Warren Bennis

Bennis just passed away in 2014 at the age of eighty-nine. During his full life, he was a decorated war hero, a senior academic, a prolific author of twenty-seven books, and an advisor to four U.S. presidents. In 1996, *Forbes* magazine described him as, "the dean of leadership gurus."

The definition of the noun, "becoming," is, "The process of coming to be something or of passing into a state." And that's definitely what I think you have to do during your entire life if you intend to be a great leader, and if you plan to remain a great leader.

I read Bennis's book when it came out in 2009. By that time, I had already been a president for twenty-six years, spanning six companies; but I was still attracted to the concept of "becoming a leader." Even after all my leadership success, I believed that I still needed to learn—I still needed to be better.

Like many of the authors I have described in this chapter, Bennis reinforced some things that I already knew, but that I required constant reminders of. Things like the need to know myself better, that sometimes I had to ignore the analytics and go with my gut instinct, and the need to focus constantly on "forging the future."

18: THE 21 IRREFUTABLE LAWS OF LEADERSHIP: FOLLOW THEM AND PEOPLE WILL FOLLOW YOU

John Maxwell

I love the original 1998 edition of this book and have not had a chance to pick up the updated 10th anniversary edition. I chose to open my first book, *Dream Job*, with a quote from Maxwell's book, "Leadership develops daily, not in a day," because I strongly believe that being a great leader truly is a lifelong journey. Today, Maxwell is one of the bestselling authors on leadership in the world, with over sixteen million books sold. To put that in context, an author has to sell only about ten thousand books to have a bestseller in Canada.

In his writings, Maxwell has passed on learning from a broad range of fields: business, politics, sports, religion, and the military. He has translated that experience into twenty-one laws, such as the Law of Process, the Law of Intuition, the Law of Empowerment, the Law of Victory, and seventeen more. Incidentally, his book title did not influence the title of this book. It was only after I started going through my personal library that I realized I had picked a similar, but still different, approach to talking about leadership. I will call it legitimate plagiarism.

19: THE POWER OF MORE: HOW SMALL STEPS CAN HELP YOU ACHIEVE BIG GOALS
Marnie McBean

I met Olympian and author Marnie McBean a few times over the years and, of course, I witnessed her dramatic Olympic victories on television. I knew that she had written a book, but I had not yet read it. One night I was having dinner with Toronto's chief city planner, Jennifer Keesmaat, and she raved about McBean's book. She said, "You have to read Marnie's 'jammed cat theory.'" So I went out and purchased the book the next day.

Naturally her book talks about preparing for and winning at the highest level in sports. As I read the book, I learned that she started rowing at age sixteen and became North America's most decorated rower, with six World and Olympic gold medals, four silvers, and two bronzes. She "won" like many successful leaders "win" in their respective fields. By working harder and doing a little bit more than her competition. By being personally happy with her results, but not satisfied with her performance. And always being committed and accountable. I am not going to give away the "jammed cat theory;" you will have to read her book to learn about that, and her belief in "the power of more."

20: THE GIRL WHO LOVED TOM GORDON
Stephen King

A strange book to be on my recommended reading list? I think not. Reading books and articles on leadership, watching TED talks, and going to conferences are good, but you can't always be focusing on just one subject if you want to be a broad-based leader and avoid getting stale. I try regularly to read fiction or history books among all my business reading. And one of my go-to authors is Stephen King.

I have read *The Stand* three times, and the 2014 Ebola outbreak in Africa made that story more true to life than I liked. His book *11/22/63* is a fictional account of preventing President Kennedy's assassination in Dallas. I remember that November 22nd day so clearly and often wonder how the world would have changed if Kennedy had lived. My point here is that you can definitely pick up ideas from non-leadership books too.

When I retired from MLSE, the company threw an outstanding retirement party for me (thanks, Barb Weinberg). I knew that I would be asked to speak and wanted my remarks to be special. I talked about a number of our accomplishments and thanked my board, my staff, and friends for all the support they had given me over my career. I also talked about how difficult a job the MLSE role was, given the public nature of our sports teams and having media and fans constantly coming at you.

In *The Girl Who Loved Tom Gordon*, the young heroine is being chased through the woods by a bear (or a monster—King always keeps the reader guessing); but in the end the girl is saved when the bear is shot by a hunter. King wrote, "Sometimes the bear gets you . . . other times one gets the bear." I decided to use that quote in my speech because it really captured my relationship with the media and the social network community. Who knows? Maybe it was the only time Stephen King has ever been quoted in a retirement speech.

21: DREAM JOB: MY WILD RIDE ON THE CORPORATE SIDE WITH THE LEAFS, THE RAPTORS AND TFC
Richard Peddie

Come on, now—you know I have to recommend my own book, *Dream Job*. Not to do so would be like not voting for yourself in an election. As the cover of my book says, it's about "my wild ride on the corporate side, with the Leafs, the Raptors and TFC." However, the book also talks in depth about my twenty-nine-year journey of "getting my ticket punched" so that I could eventually realize my dream job of running an NBA team. It's full of lessons learned, and lots of business and sports anecdotes to bring the points alive. Shameless Plug: The book is still available in paperback and online.

• • • • •

That's twenty-one books for you to consider. Just twenty-one out of all the great books ever published. Now, you might complain, "Boy, Peddie, some of those books are old." And, yes, some of them are; but what I have done is list the ones that impacted me the most over my career. More than likely, some of my twenty-one favourite books will not work for you, but I sure know that you would benefit from a few of them. And I know that people like Marnie McBean and Paul Alofs would appreciate the sales.

Today there are multiple new leadership books coming out every day, and it's impossible to keep up with them all, no matter how good they might be. For example, I have not read *Giving Voice to Values*, by Mary Gentile, but I understand she has written about how one stands up for their values when they are under pressure. Something that might really resonate with me. I also have *The Talent Code*, by Daniel Coyle, on my reading list because he has written about how greatness isn't born—it's grown. And there are countless others I'm looking forward to reading. My advice to you is to seek out both the old and the new, to discover the books that can help you create your own leadership narrative.

Often when I am giving leadership speeches today, I am asked if I had a mentor. While Paul Godfrey, Larry Tanenbaum, and other leaders have been a big help to my career, I don't believe I have ever had a true mentor. Instead, I believe that books have been my mentor, so if you don't have a mentor, or wish to have an additional one, then maybe books can be your mentor, too.

The final word on the benefit of reading books goes to American civil rights leader, John Lewis: "Reading is a liberating force. Reading will free your spirit. Reading can help you grow, help you understand this little planet."

LESSON 11

EARNED RECOGNITION

WHEN I TAUGHT "STRATEGIC LEADERSHIP" (the forerunner of my MLSE Elite Training course) at the Odette School of Business at the University of Windsor in 2001, I was introduced to the concept of "earned recognition" by professor Harold Musson, who had taught me accounting when I was a student there.

One day after one of my lectures I had lunch with Professor Musson and asked him for some advice. I had recently marked the mid-term exams for one of my classes and a student had come to me to lobby for a better grade. The individual had a long, sad story about feeling ill . . . no time to study . . . mark unfair . . . yada yada. I asked Harold what he thought about that and he told me, "The student earned the mark you gave him." From that point on, I put Harold's remark about "earned recognition" into my leadership vocabulary.

Over the next thirteen years that I led MLSE, I used the expression many times. Often when I sent out a thank-you note, or personally thanked someone for doing something special, the individual would in turn thank me. To which I quickly replied, "No need to thank me—you earned it." Sometimes people would modestly push back and say they did not deserve the reward, but I knew differently. This kind of recognition is critical to keeping employees engaged, to making them feel appreciated for their efforts and contributions—and it is so easy to do. You just have to take the time to notice and to say thank you. Such a simple act of everyday kindness, but with huge, positive implications for your business.

One of best examples of a person resisting earned recognition was Detroit Tigers star outfielder, Al Kaline. I loved watching Kaline play and contribute to the Tigers' World Series win in 1968. But when the organization wanted to increase his salary from $95,000 to $100,000 in 1970, he turned it down because he felt he did not deserve it. I do not imagine you will ever experience this type of push back when you are trying to reward an employee for a job well done, but who knows? I sure am confident that no professional athlete would ever turn down such a raise today, unless they think it is not nearly high enough.

• • • • •

There are lots of bosses who don't give much recognition, or any at all, to their employees, and that is a failure of leadership. At the same time, there are lots of leaders and institutions that give it out way too easily. Giving trophies to all the players on all the Atom or Novice division sports teams is not earned recognition and, even worse, teaches kids that there will be awards even if they do not perform well. Similarly, I believe that in business a merit-based philosophy and earned recognition go hand in hand and are the best way to lead employees.

Consistent with Lesson 8, you actually have to have edge when meting out recognition. If you do give it out too easily, with no real rationale, it will be far less effective and people will quickly learn that it is pablum and not of any real value. However, if it is given in a timely fashion (catch them in the act of doing something good) and the recognition is quite specific and personal, it will have a very positive impact.

The other key to recognition is mixing up the way you give it. In Lesson 17 I make a strong case for handwritten thank-you notes because they are very effective. But I would often add extra value to the recognition by including a pair of Leaf tickets or a bottle of wine. Even less expensive ideas, or things that cost nothing at all, can be equally effective in taking recognition up a notch; something as simple as a personal visit to someone's work station, or a mention of their excellent work on the MLSE intranet site could make an employee feel really special and much appreciated.

"The other key to recognition is mixing up the way you give it."

Later, in Lesson 16, I talk about another opportunity to give recognition—by walking the talk, you have the opportunity to call your staff by name, or ask them directly for their ideas and concerns.

When I led MLSE, we had the best corporate recognition plan that I ever participated in. We handed out awards monthly to people who lived our four corporate values; and at the end of the year we awarded a Rookie of the Year, Coach of the Year, MVP of the Year, and All-Star Team awards. And that was to the business units, not the sports teams! Unlike the awards I saw handed out at General Foods and Hostess, MLSE's annual award winners all earned their recognition.

Done right, recognition has an incredibly positive impact on the individual or team and, therefore, on the organization. As the late African-American poet, Maya Angelou, said so perfectly, "People will forget what you said, people will forget what you did, but people will never forget how you made them feel."

LESSON 12

NO SURPRISES

SURPRISING YOUR BOSSES IS NEVER A GOOD IDEA. Bad surprises can be very dangerous, but even large, good surprises can also be a problem. Ironically, even a major positive surprise may cause your boss to think that you don't know what is going on in your organization.

Just one very bad surprise can get you fired, and a string of them will definitely get you fired. Now, obviously the best defence is never to have bad news. However, you aren't realistically going to be able to avoid having bad surprises during your career. So it's up to you to know how to handle them.

Bad news never gets better with age, so when it does happen, do not try to hide it, and definitely avoid the "five stages of grief" (denial, anger, bargaining, depression and acceptance). In fact, go right to "acceptance." Disclose that you have a problem. Explain it, and move immediately to taking positive steps to overcome it. It also might be a good time to admit some personal fallibility. Own the problem, resolve the problem, and never be the type of boss who passes the blame to another department or your staff. I guarantee you will earn respect for courage and professional maturity by taking responsibility.

> **"Admit some personal fallibility. Own the problem. Resolve the problem."**

• • • • •

Now, not all surprises are bad news. Senior management or your immediate bosses will also be surprised when you suddenly declare that you are going to make an investment or a positive personnel move that they have never been previously briefed on and that they are hearing about for the first time.

At MLSE, we effectively used our annual strategic plan to give our owners a heads-up on where we wanted to take the company. We would often identify a long-term opportunity and reflect it in our out-years planning calendar and financials (revenue, expenses, and capital resources). For instance, we explained and quantified our plans for our TFC training centre in a couple of strategic plans before we asked for approval to go ahead with it. Same with many major capital improvements to Air Canada Centre.

Through our long-range plans, our board became comfortable with our intentions to expand BMO Field. They knew that we would want to invest the capital dollars once the team made the playoffs. In all cases, when the time did come to ask for the resources, the board was not surprised and securing approval was easy. In every case we explained our thinking, sensitized them to the idea, and moved them gradually towards a decision. I love good, long-range strategic plans for the way that they can get all parties moving effectively towards common objectives.

Now, I am not suggesting you take months and years to make every decision, because today the world seldom allows you that luxury. Sometimes the heads-up might only be days before you need to discuss a pressing issue with your boss. Again, at MLSE we circulated our presentations to the board at least a week in advance. To make sure every board member was up to speed, Ian Clarke, my chief financial officer, or I would contact most of the board members to see if they had any early questions or concerns. I always made a point of sitting down before our board meetings with our chairman, Larry

Tanenbaum, to flip through the pages of the presentation to understand what he was thinking.

Getting the deck out in advance and looking for early feedback gave my team a heads-up regarding any issues. Sometimes when we heard the board's concerns in advance, we prepared more supporting materials before the actual meeting. Other times, frankly, we lobbied, which wasn't always popular; but it increased our chance of getting the board to agree.

Paul Godfrey, a very experienced and successful leader, once told me that one should never go into a board meeting without knowing how everyone was going to vote. I explained and listened before every board meeting because I did not want to surprise my board, and, equally important, I did not want to be surprised either. A classic example of "forewarned is forearmed."

• • • • •

Bosses and boards aren't the only ones who should not be surprised. As much as you can, don't surprise your employees either. If your business is having problems, make sure your employees know that. Bring them into the tent to get their ideas and motivate them to help out with the solution.

"Don't surprise your employees either."

And when it comes to performance issues with employees, heed the advice in Lesson 8: Be candid and thorough with your employee about any negative or corrective feedback you might have. Identifying their development needs may allow them to course-correct and improve their performance. Keeping them in the dark gives them no opportunity to turn things around and exposes the company to possible legal action if they are ever terminated. So employees should never be completely surprised about being let go. Shocked maybe, but not surprised.

No leader can completely avoid surprising their bosses and their employees. But through timely communications and quick action you can almost always mitigate the potential damage that can come from unexpected news. Nonetheless, it's best that you do not make surprising your colleagues and your bosses a frequent practice.

LESSON 13

WHAT GETS MEASURED GETS DONE

THERE ARE COUNTLESS VERSIONS OF THE EXPRESSION, "What gets measured gets done." Similar expressions are, "What gets measured gets managed," "To measure is to know," Some even say, "What doesn't get measured doesn't get done." There is debate over who first expressed this idea, and we really don't know who it was. One possible original source of the concept may be the Scottish physicist, Lord Kelvin, who said in 1883, "I often say that when you can measure what you are speaking about and express it in numbers, you know something about it; but when you cannot express it in numbers, your knowledge is of meagre and unsatisfactory kind . . . ."

Today companies depend and thrive on analytics more than ever before. I am not suggesting that you have to be a stats wizard to succeed, but you sure should be comfortable with all kinds of business metrics.

From an early age, I liked data. Not math, mind you, but data. I read Detroit Tigers batting and pitching statistics religiously, had my bird count list, and even kept track of how many and what kind of fish I caught on vacation.

My best example of using measurement to accomplish a personal goal was in long-distance running. About the same time I began dreaming about running a basketball team, I also decided that I wanted to run the Boston Marathon. I started training in university, but did not get really serious about qualifying until my late twenties. Back then, the qualifying time for men under forty was under three hours (not the wimpy 3:10 it is today). My first marathon was a respectable 3:46 in Ottawa, but still forty-six minutes short of qualifying for the Boston race. In 1981, I ran under three hours in the Toronto marathon and thought I had made it. Boston in turn lowered their qualifying time to 2:50 (see how wimpy 3:10 is today?). So instead of giving up, I just dedicated myself to training harder.

Intervals on Tuesday and Thursday, time trial on Saturday, twenty-mile runs on Sunday—all adding up to over sixty-five miles a week and over 3,000 miles a year. And not only was I measuring distance, but I was also tracking my racing times, my weight, body-fat composition, my resting and running pulse rate. It all paid off in 1983, as I ran the Detroit Marathon in 2:46 and qualified for Boston the next spring. I absolutely know that I would never have been able to qualify for Boston without measuring my progress. When I ended my racing career ten years later, I realized that I appreciated that Boston had made it tougher for me to qualify because it stretched me to run even faster.

While I had an early personal affinity for measurement, what really got it going was when I worked in the market research department at Colgate. There, I learned about attitude surveys, product home-use tests, top box scores, and the importance of empirical research. Today, a lot of what you hear about is actually only anecdotal research. For instance, the television newscast that merely interviews three people and portrays it as what everyone is thinking about a certain story. Now, I do think there is role to play for focus groups, monitoring social media sites, and reading comments to the editor; but one needs to realize that those sources are only directional at their very best.

Due to my early experience at Colgate, I took a more scientific market research bias to all of the companies that I led. At MLSE we did quantitative research on season seat- and suite-holders, sponsors, employees, and even what the community was thinking about us. Armed with this data, we made decisions on what strategies we should use to strengthen or correct the negative things we were learning about.

• • • • •

In the last couple of years, another form of "what gets measured gets done" has become the rage in some sports: analytics. In one form or another, analytics has been around for years, but gained increased popularity when Billy Beane, general manager of baseball's Oakland A's, started having on-field success due to his prolific and disciplined use of statistics to evaluate player performance and make personnel decisions (this type of statistical analysis is now known as sabermetrics). Then the book *Money Ball*, by Michael Lewis, and the spin-off movie starring Brad Pitt, put Billy Beane and analytics on every fan's radar screen.

The Houston Rockets' Daryl Morey was one of the first NBA general managers who started using statistics in this way: "Analytics helps you make better decisions," he declared. And today Morey is the chairperson of the annually sold-out MIT Sloan Sports Analytics Conference. In 2015, over 3,000 people, including attendees from 100 teams, were at the event. Bill Simmons (formerly of ESPN, Grantland, and currently at HBO) now refers to the conference as "dorkapalooza."

Not everyone in the sports world has been quick to adopt analytics, nor is everyone even a fan of them today. I remember starting to push for MLSE's use of analytics over a decade ago, and actually received anonymous criticism from one of our board members in my annual performance review for doing so. It took

Brian Colangelo, former general manager of the Raptors, a long time before he started paying attention to the numbers in a big way, and the Leafs really did not embrace analytics until Brendan Shanahan came on board as president in 2014.

And even today analytics still have some very vocal critics, like Charles Barkley, former NBA player and now a TV sports analyst. I love listening to Charles—so outrageous, so funny. Early in 2015, he went on air and ripped Morey for his reliance on analytics and described all the proponents of analytics as, "a bunch of guys who never played the game, and never got the girls in high school." Barkley closed his critique with, "I've always believed analytics was crap." The irony is that Barkley was once one of the NBA's top power forwards and if one looks at the analytics on him over the course of his career, they are excellent.

I do believe that sports analytics are a bit of a "flavour of the month," and are viewed as a panacea by many a losing team. Now, don't get me wrong, I believe that analytics play a valuable role in helping build a winner, but they are just one variable. To me, they are best used along with other important variables, like fitness and skills measurements, game films, police checks, individual psychological test results, what the scouts have observed, and (because often the best predictor of future behaviour is past behaviour) how the individual has behaved with teammates and in the community over the years.

• • • • •

Analytics are just as important in business as they are in sports. In fact, clearly defined metrics and quantitative analysis are critical to business success. At MLSE we clearly wanted to win

"Analytics are just as important in business as they are in sports."

on the ice, court, and pitch. Winning on the playing fields was the objective and the role of team management and players alike. At the same time, MLSE was also a big business. Admittedly a very sexy business, but a business just the same; and an important investment for all of our shareholders. So we also had to win off the playing field as well, and that was the role of the almost 700 full-time staff who worked on our business team.

Accordingly, we set company-wide annual objectives and used business analytics to track progress, measure success, and take corrective action. We had customer service standards of performance that staff were responsible for hitting. Our sales and service people had revenue targets that their sales incentives were based on. Across the company, leaders were judged, in part, on how their department scored on our employee attitude survey. We took the numbers so seriously that every non-union employee, including me, participated in a bonus plan based on MLSE'S annual results as determined by the company's bottom-line profits.

As a leader, I have always been a champion of having clear, measurable personal, team, and organizational objectives. Over the years, I have read numerous studies that document the merit of formulating these kinds of goals at every level in the company. For instance, a *Forbes* article by Ashley Feinstein described a 1979 study in which graduate students in the Harvard MBA program were asked, "Have you set clear, written goals for your future and made plans to accomplish them?" The result:

> "Only 3% had written goals and plans, 13% had goals but they weren't in writing and 84% had no goals at all. Ten years later . . . the 13% of the class who had goals, but did not write them down was earning twice the amount of the 84% who had no goals. The 3% who had written goals were earning, on average, ten times as much as the other 97% of the class combined."

More than enough proof for me.

Today I am completely satisfied that what gets written down and what gets measured helps gets things done. That approach worked at MLSE. It helped me qualify for the Boston marathon, and it definitely helped me realize my basketball dream. It can work for you, too, in just about anything you choose to do in life.

LESSON 14

MONUMENTS ARE NOT ERECTED FOR PESSIMISTS

THE LATE RADIO BROADCASTER with the distinctive voice, Paul Harvey, once said, "I've never seen a monument erected for a pessimist." While I cannot prove that Harvey is correct, I do agree with him. Personally, I am an optimist by nature and I believe that all leaders need to be as well to be successful.

Now, I am not suggesting that one should practice "head in the sand, wear rose-coloured glasses, don't worry be happy" optimism. No, I believe that one should always be strategic, do the proper research, be mindful of current best practices, execute superbly—and then you have every reason to be optimistic. And more often than not you will be successful. In other words, hope itself is not a strategy, but if you put a lot of solid strategies in place and execute superbly, then you can be optimistic about your organization's future—and yours.

Martin Seligman, a founder of the positive psychology movement, believes that one is often optimistic about their beliefs or their expectations for the future because of their past experiences with success. During my career, my past successes very much encouraged me to be optimistic about future ones. Vision and values worked so well at Pillsbury, I was optimistic that they would work at SkyDome and MLSE. Using the disciplined approach to business analysis that the consumer products industry taught me, I analyzed football's potential in Toronto, and that convinced me TFC would be successful. The experience I had at NetStar working on TSN and the Discovery Channel made me optimistic that Leafs TV and Raptors TV would work. Sure, I had my doubts along the way and, yes, I had to fight off the pessimists and naysayers every time, but my general optimism carried me through.

• • • • •

There has been a lot of research on this subject over the last thirty years, and I know that anyone who disagrees with me can easily find many studies and articles that caution against the theory of positive psychology. For instance, if you are a non-believer, just Google the *New York Times* article by Gabriele Oettingen, "The Problem with Positive Thinking," or her article in the *Harvard Business Review*, "Stop Being So Positive." Oettingen strongly believes that optimists make the same or less progress in achieving their goals as those who are not optimists. And in his book, *The Hard Thing About Hard Things*, author Ben Horowitz claims that his biggest single improvement as CEO occurred when he stopped being too positive. Fair enough, but neither Oettingen nor Horowitz speaks for me on this subject.

I almost included the book *It Worked for Me*, by General Colin Powell, in Lesson 10 in this book. In it, he outlines thirteen rules of leadership, and one of them is the need for optimism. As he puts it:

> "Perpetual Optimism is a Force Multiplier—the ripple effect of a leader's enthusiasm and optimism is awesome. So is the impact of cynicism and pessimism. Leaders who whine and blame engender those same behaviors among their colleagues. I am not talking about stoically accepting organizational stupidity and performance incompetence with a 'what me worry' smile. I am talking about a gung-ho attitude that says 'we can change things here, we can achieve awesome

> goals, we can be the best.' Spare me the grim litany of the 'realist,' give me the unrealistic aspirations of the optimist any day."

During my life I have been lucky to be surrounded by optimistic people. My brother, Tom, always sees the positive side of any challenge or issue. My University of Windsor classmate, Mike Mueller, was the one who got our entire graduating class saying, "Excellent!" when we were asked how we were doing. I never met Hall of Famer Ernie Banks of the Chicago Cubs, but I sure wish I had, and his positive attitude influenced me nonetheless. Growing up, Banks had to battle through a lot. His father played semi-pro baseball in the Texas black leagues, picked cotton, and worked hard as a janitor in a grocery chain to support his family of twelve kids. Banks became the Cubs' first black player in 1953, and went on to be one of greatest power-hitting shortstops in the history of Major League Baseball. People say he was an unconquerable optimist and that was best expressed by his mantra, "It's a beautiful day for a ballgame. Let's play two."

"Unfortunately, my optimism never helped our teams at MLSE win it all, or even win enough."

Unfortunately, my optimism never helped our teams at MLSE win it all, or even win enough; but I am convinced that without my optimistic leadership MLSE would never have become a two-billion-dollar sports and entertainment giant. I definitely encourage you to be an optimist, but make sure your optimism is always accompanied by solid strategic thinking, creativity, and superb execution.

LESSON 15

21 OF MY FAVOURITE QUOTES

I STARTED COLLECTING QUOTES IN MY JOURNAL in university. The same journal in which I wrote about my basketball dream. During that time I wrote down quotes that I liked from newspapers, books, songs—all kinds of places. As I started moving through my career, I found that quotes could be an effective way to reinforce an idea I was supporting. When I started giving speeches I found quotes to be a very powerful way to make my point and leave a positive impression.

I highly recommend that you follow a similar practice. Writing down meaningful quotes or ideas from others can provide you with inspiration for years to come, in your career and in your life in general. Collecting quotes that inspire you can also help you to see patterns in terms of the ideas that consistently appeal to you and the core values that are fundamental touchstones in your life. And when you hit a rough patch or a particularly challenging time in your career, reviewing the quotes you've collected over the years can help to keep you on track, remind you of what's most important to you, and motivate you to keep going.

Following are some of my favourites from over the years and the backstory behind each one of them. Unlike the quotes in my later "Bonus" chapter (where all the quotes are my own, and ones you might not want to hang onto anyway), I have given credit here where credit is available and due. I hope you'll find some of these quotations worthy of adding to your own collection, and that you'll have some fun gathering others that appeal to you along the way.

• • • • •

1: "BE DARING, BE DIFFERENT, BE FIRST."

—Unknown

When I took over Pillsbury it was a company with great quality brands and lots of low-hanging fruit, but it was asleep at the switch. Our team badly needed to jump-start the company. Specifically, we had to increase our share of market, increase sales, and grow profits. Accordingly, we decided to be a much more aggressive company with many new product introductions, new sales and employee initiatives, plus we made a couple acquisitions of other companies. This quote was our proud rallying call, and it worked. On every metric, Pillsbury grew and became a much better company.

2: "STANDING STILL IS NOT AN OPTION."

—Variation of a Chinese proverb

This was an approach that I followed at all the companies I led. I knew that technology, the marketplace, and our competitors were not standing still, so neither could we. When I took over the Leafs I initially got real pushback from our part-time event staff about improvements we wanted to make in fan service. After much training, communication, and encouragement, they got on board. Herminia Ibarra just published a book, entitled *Act Like a Leader, Think Like a Leader*, in which she writes about the need for leaders to react to today's breakneck pace of change. She recently spoke at Rotman and I am sorry I missed hearing her.

3: "THE BEST TIME TO PLANT A TREE WAS TWENTY YEARS AGO. THE SECOND BEST TIME IS RIGHT NOW."

—Japanese proverb

I used this quote the first time I spoke to the Windsor Chamber of Commerce, where I championed the need to protect the beautiful but fragile natural environment of Essex county in southern Ontario. I strongly believe that climate change is happening and I know that planting young trees is a way to capture some of the 100 million tonnes of carbon dioxide (CO_2) that is going up into the atmosphere every year. On our Boblo Island property, where the Detroit River empties into Lake Erie, we have planted over 100 new trees that look beautiful and now attract hundreds of birds and animals to a safe natural environment. The lesson from that old proverb is that there's no time like the present to change a situation. However, if you have missed out on an opportunity to do something in the past, taking action now is better than not doing anything it all.

4: "OUR CHIEF WANT IS SOMEONE WHO WILL INSPIRE US TO BE WHAT WE KNOW WE COULD BE."

—Ralph Waldo Emerson, 19th century American essayist, lecturer, and poet

In university classes I teach today, I often ask what makes a great leader. Despite their young age and limited work experience, the students pretty much already know the yin and yang of great leadership. For instance they know that good communication skills are important. That leaders should be honest and that bullying is not acceptable. After discussing the traits of good and bad leaders, I tell them that I hope they get the chance to work for inspiring leaders during their career. I also remind them that some day they are going to be leaders who, in turn, will have an obligation to inspire the people who will work for them someday.

5: "THE VERY ESSENCE OF LEADERSHIP IS THAT YOU HAVE TO HAVE A VISION. YOU CAN'T BLOW AN UNCERTAIN TRUMPET."

—Theodore Hesburgh, former president of the University of Notre Dame

Basically, if you have values that support your vision, you have to adhere to them. Not just when it is convenient or profitable to do so. A leader has to have the courage to make tough decisions consistent with their corporate and personal values. If a leader makes a decision that goes against one of the company's core values, then he or she threatens the legitimacy of having corporate values at all. As Yoda said in *The Empire Strikes Back*, "Do. Or do not. There is no try."

6: "THE RIVER I STEP INTO IS NOT THE RIVER I STAND IN."

—Greek Philosopher Heraclitus

I came across this quote when I was out running one day. The quote is written in the steelwork of the Queen Street bridge crossing the Don River in Toronto. I used this quote in my Elite Training program at MLSE when we were discussing strategic plans. I always asked the class what they thought it meant. Only a few in the class ever linked this quote to the importance of frequently adjusting a company's strategic plan to keep up with the times. I wonder—what does stepping into the river mean to you?

7: "ONLY WHEN YOU GET INTO THE PROBLEM, AND THE PROBLEM BECOMES CLEAR, CAN CREATIVITY TAKE OVER."

—Charles Eames, an American designer who made major contributions to modern architecture and furniture

I love Eames's design work. I also love the fact that early on in his career his approach to architecture was dismissed as "too modern" and that he had to fight through a lot of criticism before his contributions in modern architecture and furniture were recognized. I like this quote because I have always found that once I really grasp a problem, the solution often becomes quite apparent.

We have an Eames chair in our Toronto den and my wife, Colleen, does some of her best business thinking in it. That is, when she is not doing math puzzles online.

8: "WILL YOU PLAY IT SAFE OR WILL YOU BE A LITTLE SWASHBUCKLING? WHEN IT IS TOUGH WILL YOU GIVE UP OR WILL YOU BE RELENTLESS? WILL YOU BE A CYNIC OR WILL YOU BE A BUILDER? WILL YOU BE CLEVER AT THE EXPENSE OF OTHERS OR WILL YOU BE KIND?"

—Jeff Bezos, Founder and CEO of Amazon

I don't like how Amazon is treating authors and publishers, because publishing is tough enough without a major distributor squeezing their profits, but I do admire Bezos for creating a company that does not seem to make money yet is valued at over $240 billion. I am also watching with interest to see if he turns around the *Washington Post*. If he is successful with the *Post*, it might be an instructive best practice for many of the world's ailing newspapers. I have used Bezos's quote at the end of many of my speeches at business schools and universities because it touches on many of the things I believe in. Taking risks. Fighting through adversity. Being a builder and, most importantly in the end, being kind. Now I just hope you can purchase this book on Amazon.

9: "EVEN IF YOU DO NOT REALIZE YOUR DREAM, YOU WILL ACCOMPLISH MUCH FROM TRYING."

—Unknown

I have often been asked by students what I would have felt if I hadn't realized my basketball dream. I have always told them that even if I had failed to become president of an NBA team, I would have been proud of all the other successes I had leading companies, developing future leaders, and contributing to the communities I have lived in.

10: "IT'S THE POSSIBILITY OF HAVING A DREAM COME TRUE THAT MAKES LIFE INTERESTING."

—Paulo Coelho, Brazilian lyricist and novelist

Most people are familiar with the old Chinese proverb that says, "May you live in interesting times." And I'm sure many know that the Chinese context of the word "interesting" means dangerous or turbulent, thus making the proverb's wish something of a curse. I am sure that this is not what Coelho intended to mean. Instead he views "interesting" as a positive development. My career was often turbulent, and even a little dangerous if you count the death threats; but it was interesting in the most positive ways too.

11: "A VISION WITHOUT ACTION IS A DAYDREAM. ACTION WITHOUT VISION IS A NIGHTMARE."

—Japanese proverb

I have repeated this quote here from earlier in the book because it is so true. Today, lots of companies have a vision statement but really don't live it. Or, to use an example from municipal government, during Rob Ford's time as mayor of Toronto it was clear he had no real vision for the city ("End the gravy train" is not a vision) and, accordingly, his initiatives were all over the map and from many perspectives a nightmare (even without the personal scandals factored in). I smiled when I heard that San Jose Sharks GM, Doug Wilson, also used this quote in a meeting with season-ticket holders near the end of the 2014-15 season—I guess the quote is gaining some traction.

12: "WE WILL GET WHAT WE EXPECT FROM THE PLAYERS. IF WE SET THE BAR LOW, WE WILL GET LOW BEHAVIOR FROM OUR PLAYERS ON AND OFF THE COURT. IF WE SET THE BAR HIGH, WE WILL GET THEIR BEST BEHAVIOR."

—David Stern, former commissioner of the NBA, and Billy Hunter, past executive director of the National Basketball Players Association

At an NBA governors' meeting at the end of the 1999 lockout, both Commissioner Stern and NBPA Director, Billy Hunter, addressed the thirty team governors and they talked about how we could all get the best out of our players when it came to working with sponsors, fans, media, and the community. This quote from them resonated with me and I find that it is equally relevant to anyone leading business teams.

In fact, this quote encouraged me to create a "Business of Basketball" presentation for the Raptors players. A presentation that stressed the importance of the fans and sponsorships and that, when all was said and done, it was their spending that paid the player salaries. After a couple of years the league became aware of it and made the presentation mandatory for all teams. Over the years we got much better with how we presented this message to the players, but I will always remember Tracy McGrady falling asleep in the only one he attended. I guess it will never interest all of the players who hear it!

13: "LEADERSHIP DOESN'T DEVELOP IN A DAY, IT TAKES A LIFETIME."

—John Maxwell,bestselling author and speaker on leadership

One of the messages I constantly preach to young leaders is, if they want to be great leaders, their journey will last their entire life, and that they definitely cannot expect to become a good leader right away. I also tell them that they can't sit passively back and wait to be a great leader; instead they have to invest time and work hard work at it. At the Odette School of Business at the University of Windsor, there is a Leadership Learning Centre named after me. On the wall leading into the classroom is an inscription inspired by Maxwell's quote: "Becoming a great leader is a lifelong journey."

14: TRYING TO PREDICT THE FUTURE IS LIKE TRYING TO DRIVE DOWN A COUNTRY ROAD AT NIGHT WITH NO LIGHTS ON WHILE LOOKING IN THE REAR WINDOW."

—Peter Drucker, American management consultant and thought leader

Peter Drucker is one of the greatest business and leadership gurus of all time, and if you Google Drucker quotes, you'll find many excellent ones. I chose this one in particular because I think it describes the challenge of creating good strategic plans. My early strategic planning experience in the consumer products industry was not very good. Those plans were thrown together with not much thought given to their actual content or the financial forecasts that backed them up.

When I introduced strategic plans at MLSE, my intention was to create really actionable plans with solid numbers behind them. Henry Mintzberg, a well know author and academic, contends that "only ten percent of most companies' actions arise out of their strategic planning." At MLSE, that was not our experience at all and our batting average was very high. The strategic ideas MLSE created in its football, broadcast, and real estate businesses were instrumental in dramatically growing enterprise value.

15: "FOR EVERY ACTION THERE IS AN EQUAL AND OPPOSITE REACTION."

—Sir Isaac Newton, English physicist and mathematician and one of the most influential scientists of his time

Who knew that physics would apply to leadership? Well, it clearly does. Negative reaction to a constructive evaluation, or someone's lack of follow-through on a commitment, are both examples of Newton's Third Law of Motion in the workplace. The point is that every action you take will cause a reaction from someone else, whether you intend it to or not. To try to get this concept through to young business students, I use examples of engaging with websites and social media, where a young person does something regrettable and it's captured and shared broadly for all to see. I remind them that any of their less-than-favourable Vine and Facebook postings, or YouTube videos, might be discovered one day by a human resources department doing due diligence on the individual's suitability for employment. And remember, those digital images never disappear.

Also remember that every action has consequences, and they might not be the type of reaction you want, or ever imagined, so be mindful in everything you do and say.

16: "DON'T TRY TO BE PERFECT. INFLUENCE OTHERS BY SHOWING THAT YOU DON'T HAVE ALL THE ANSWERS."

—Dr. Richard Davis, management consultant and bestselling author

This quote is out of Davis's book, *The Intangibles of Leadership*, and concludes his chapter on "Fallibility." I got a lot out of his book; so much, in fact, that I've included it in Lesson 10 as one of the books I recommend that you read. As a leader, I made a fair number of mistakes during my career. All leaders are sure to do the same. It's all part of learning and developing. Thankfully my good decisions outweighed my bad ones.

Easily my worst business decision at MLSE was agreeing to a twenty-year, no-outs agreement with the City of Toronto to lease Ricoh Coliseum at Exhibition Place as the home arena for our American Hockey League professional hockey team, the Toronto Marlies. Having the Marlies play in Toronto costs MLSE about seven million dollars annually. The rationale to move the Leafs' AHL franchise to Toronto continues to be very solid for MLSE, the fans, and the players alike; but the lease price I agreed to on the arena is way over what the market now says it is worth.

I was not proud of the lousy deal I negotiated with the city, but I did not run from that decision either. Each year I fully disclosed the financial losses to the MLSE board and talked about how we were working hard to remedy them. The last time I presented to the board, they heard me out and said, "Richard, we get it. Continue to try to reduce the losses, but you don't need to bring it up again."

Today I am pleased to hear that the Montreal Canadiens and Winnipeg Jets plan to move their AHL clubs to their home cities for the same reasons we did (mainly strategic player development and salary cap management).

I strongly believe that good leaders have to own up to their fallibilities. I know I was candid about my mistakes in my own book, *Dream Job*, and I continue to be candid about my fallibilities when I am delivering speeches or giving interviews.

When you make your own inevitable mistakes, will you go through the "five stages of grief" or admit your shortcomings and get on with the steps to correct the problem?

**17: "SUCCESS IS IN THE WAY YOU WALK
THE PATHS OF LIFE EACH DAY;
IT IS IN THE LITTLE THINGS YOU DO,
AND IN THE THINGS YOU SAY;
SUCCESS IS IN THE GLAD HELLO
YOU GIVE YOUR FELLOW MAN;
IT'S IN THE LAUGHTER OF YOUR HOME
AND ALL THE JOYS YOU PLAN.**

**"SUCCESS IS NOT IN GETTING RICH
OR RISING HIGH TO FAME;
IT'S NOT ALONE IN WINNING GOALS,
WHICH PEOPLE HOPE TO CLAIM;
IT'S IN THE MAN YOU ARE EACH DAY,
THROUGH HAPPINESS OR CARE;
IT'S IN THE CHEERY WORDS YOU SPEAK
AND IN THE SMILE YOU WEAR.**

**"SUCCESS IS BEING BIG OF HEART AND
CLEAN AND BROAD IN MIND;
IT'S BEING FAITHFUL TO YOUR FRIENDS
AND TO STRANGERS, KIND;
IT'S IN THE CHILDREN WHOM YOU LOVE,
AND ALL THEY LEARN FROM YOU—
SUCCESS DEPENDS ON CHARACTER
AND EVERYTHING YOU DO."**

—Edgar Guest, American poet of the first half of the twentieth century

Over the years I have given many speeches at the University of Windsor and have often ended them with this poem. I am viewed as one of the more successful alumni of the university, but with this quote, I attempt to emphasize to students that the definition of success encompasses much more than titles and money. Many times when I have used this quote, a number of people from the audience have come up after my speech to request a copy of it.

18: "LEADERSHIP IS A COMBINATION OF STRATEGY AND CHARACTER. IF YOU MUST BE WITHOUT ONE, BE WITHOUT STRATEGY."

—General Norman Schwarzkopf, American army general who led the coalition forces in the Persian Gulf war

I believe this quote reinforces the points I made in Lesson 2 on values. I can't stress enough how important having great values is to being an excellent leader. There are lots of leaders who are very smart and their functional skills are superior, but when it comes to having great values they are a miserable failure.

19: "THE MAIN DIFFERENCE BETWEEN MANAGEMENT AND LEADERSHIP IS THAT LEADERSHIP IS ABOUT INFLUENCING PEOPLE TO FOLLOW YOU, WHILE MANAGEMENT FOCUSES ON MAINTAINING SYSTEMS AND PROCEDURES."

—John Maxwell, once again from his excellent book, The 21 Irrefutable Laws of Leadership

In Elite Training at MLSE, I really stressed the key differences between a manager and a leader. I always maintain that all leaders need to have management skills; but if that's where your skills stop, then you can never lead your people to real success. Mark Sanborn, author and leadership expert, created a chart on the nine differences between managers and leaders. For example, "Managers react to change—leaders create change," and, "Managers take credit—leaders take responsibility." It would be worth your time to reflect on the differences between managing and leading.

20: "IF YOUR ACTIONS INSPIRE OTHERS TO DREAM MORE, LEARN MORE, DO MORE AND BECOME MORE, YOU ARE A LEADER."

—John Quincy Adams, sixth president of the United States

I think this quote captures the ideal leadership journey perfectly. If you dream, learn, and invest your time, you have an excellent chance of accomplishing a great deal. In my career I accomplished just about everything that I wanted to by doing all these things. Mind you, winning a championship or two would have been nice.

21: "WHERE THERE IS NO VISION, THE PEOPLE PERISH."
—Proverbs 29:18

I am not a religious person at all, but back in 2001 when I was writing my class lessons for Odette I came across this quote. The specific lecture I was writing was on the importance of vision and values. To make my point that vision and values have a long history, I talked about this mention in the Bible; then the history of The Hudson Bay Company, starting in the seventeenth century; visionary business thinker, Walt Disney; and finally Peters's and Waterman's book, *In Search of Excellence.* My hope in sharing this brief business history was that my students would realize that the concept of vision and values was not just a passing leadership fancy.

LESSON 16

WALK THE TALK

"WALK THE TALK" is an expression you hear a lot in business. Yahoo defines it to mean, "To do as you say you would do, to be consistent with your words and action." Of course, the negative, flip side of the coin is, "Talk the talk, but don't walk it." Nothing can undermine your credibility as a leader more quickly than saying one thing and doing another. To be respected, you must be authentic; and to be authentic, you must be consistent. You must practice what you preach to be a successful leader.

"Nothing can undermine your credibility as a leader more quickly than saying one thing and doing another."

I started walking the talk long before I even knew it was a contemporary business idiom. Colgate—where I worked in sales, market research, and industrial engineering in the early part of my career—forced me to do it when they put me through their training programs. In all of those training assignments I learned some key functional skills, but I also learned how to respect and work with the people in those departments.

At Hostess I wanted to know what was going on in the grocery trade. What were the retailers thinking? What was the competition doing? What were the issues and opportunities within our salesforce? So almost weekly I worked with a sales rep, driving around together making retail calls, putting up displays, and refilling shelves. At Pillsbury I sometimes worked side by side with the workers in our plants to see exactly how Green Giant corn was processed and what were the roles of the people who did the work.

At SkyDome I took tickets at the gate when the line-ups to get in were too long. I cleaned up garbage between *Disney on Ice* shows; and once, while performing a security role, I had to tackle a fan who ran out onto the baseball field. The next week my staff presented me with a small wrestling trophy that read, "Best Tackle of the Year."

At MLSE I walked the corridors, saying hello to employees by name, talking to fans, giving seat directions, and often cleaning up tables. I did internal monthly podcasts, in which I focused on many areas of the company. One month the podcast featured me helping our Real Sports chef, Tony Glitz, prepare his famous chicken wings; in another, I interviewed members of our important cleaning staff. Initially, some of our unionized employees thought what I was doing was strange, and once I was even criticized for performing union work, but that soon all went away and everyone got used to me walking around and getting involved. In fact, at Christmas one year I received a holiday card from our window-cleaner, Jim Heeley, who described me as, "the original undercover boss."

• • • • •

I walked the talk because I wanted to know what was going on, and to get to know our people. I also did it to reinforce two of our core values: inspire our people, and excite our fans. Too many leaders walk through their office or plant and treat it like they're police at an accident scene: "Move along—nothing to see here." Too often they don't even bother to manage by walking around and, when they do, they avoid engaging with their employees and processes. Instead, I walked with the intent to learn not only what needed to be corrected, but also I wanted to come up with new ideas. I also made sure to acknowledge as many people by name as I could.

Today, many of you will work amid the noise of your jobs, trying to get better; but often you have so many distractions that you don't see what is going on all around you. And that blindness will cause you to miss out on so much. So take the time to walk around, really see what's going on, engage with the people doing the work, and constantly learn about your own business and your own organization. You'll be a better leader for leading by example.

In researching for this book I came across an article in *Psychology Today* that said that Charles Darwin, the father of evolutionary theory, was a daily walker. Every day, Darwin walked down a track near his home in England that he called his "thinking path." He found that he learned things and solved many problems on his daily stroll. I found that long-distance running had that same effect on me. And it was also my experience when I walked the talk down the many corporate halls I travelled.

LESSON 17

BE SURE TO SAY THANKS

REALLY, PEDDIE? One of your twenty-one leadership lessons is the power of sending handwritten thank-you notes?

Yes! Too analogue for you in this digital world? Shouldn't be—not at all! Some of the niceties and good, old-fashioned gestures of consideration should never get old.

Over my career I have encouraged thousands and thousands of students and young professionals to invest time sending handwritten thank-you notes. Unfortunately, probably far less than one percent of my audiences have ever paid attention and started to do it regularly. I am convinced that the other ninety-nine percent are making a big mistake.

My sister, Carol Sullivan, first encouraged me to write thank-you notes, and I did that off and on for a few years. When I started moving up the corporate ladder in General Foods, I started doing it more frequently; but it wasn't until I became president of Hostess that I made it almost an art form. I had the marketing department create cards for me, blank on the inside for handwritten notes and with our three Munchies on the cover (these monster-type creatures appeared on every chip bag and in all our ads for many years).

"During my career I wrote thousands of cards."

I did the same thing at Pillsbury, except that the Doughboy and Green Giant were on the outside. At SkyDome it was a drawing of the stadium roof open, with fireworks coming out the top. At MLSE it was the pictures of our four team logos and, for the first time, our vision and values statement on the back cover of the card. Eventually we made that card available to all our employees to use.

During my career I wrote thousands of cards. I wrote them to headhunters and interviewers, thanking them for considering me for a job. (I actually think the notes were a difference maker on a couple of job offers I received.) I wrote them to customers, thanking them for their business. I wrote them to employees, thanking them for their contribution. I also wrote them to friends and colleagues who were having success, or in some cases were having a hard time. When I left Hostess, Pillsbury, SkyDome, and MLSE, I wrote hundreds of "goodbye and thank you" notes to staff who I thought had really made a difference.

Over the last twenty years of my career, I probably wrote three cards a day, on average. Some people think it is a stupid idea and have made fun of it, but I absolutely, absolutely know it works. Writing a personal thank-you takes so little time and becomes very easy with practice, yet such a little thing makes an enormous difference to the person on the receiving end, making them feel good, appreciated, recognized.

So are you going to be one of the one percent that sends out handwritten notes? Or are you going to be one of the ninety-nine percent who do not? I guarantee that your personal notes will separate you from the clutter and make you stand out in a crowd. And each note will give the recipient insight into what kind of person you are. Of course I hope you learn something from all the lessons in this book, but, as insignificant as it may seem, this lesson could be the most personally impactful one of all.

LESSON 18

THE CHALLENGE OF WINNING IT ALL

"WINNING IT ALL" IS SIMPLY IMPOSSIBLE in business. New products fail at an alarming rate and quickly disappear from view. Records indicate that, despite thorough research by the brightest business minds, over sixty percent of all mergers and acquisitions do not meet their investment objectives. And sometimes, despite being an excellent leader, you lose your star employee to a competitor.

But despite all the challenges to winning it all, during my twenty-six-year business career—before I entered the world of professional sports—I did pretty well, winning much more than losing. When I ran Hostess and Pillsbury we had some very good years. But so did other companies like Campbell Soup, Nestlé and P&G. Winning is different in business. It's not a zero-sum game where if you don't win it all, you lose; business is all about increasing market share, exceeding your business plan, or improving your financial results versus the year before. But there are some interesting lessons for business leaders from the "win or lose" world of sports.

> **"Sports is the ultimate meritocracy."**

Many companies can have great years and view themselves as winners, even if they're not number one on every measure; but that's not true in the business of sports. You see, sports is very Darwinian and is the ultimate meritocracy. Each year in the NHL and NBA there are twenty-nine losers and one winner. As my good friend, Brian Burke, likes to say, "There is only one parade." Or, as the Clippers' all-star guard, Chris Paul, said after his team got bounced out of the 2015 playoffs by the Houston Rockets, "If you are not first, you are last."

• • • • •

Winning it all in sports is damn tough. For instance, in Toronto the Blue Jays have not been in the playoffs since 1993, the year they won the second of their back-to-back World Series championships. That's currently the longest playoff drought in the major North American professional sports. With the trade-deadline moves they made in 2015 for all-stars like David Price and Troy Tulowitzki, they are clearly trying to end that drought. By the time you read this book, we will have seen if their strategy to win it all worked. The Raptors have never gone beyond the first round of the playoffs. In their existence, TFC has never even made the playoffs. And, of course, everyone knows that the Leafs have not won the Stanley Cup since 1967.

When it comes to sports and "winning it all," I am not talking about winning more games than you lose. Nor am I talking about simply making the playoffs. No, I am talking about actually winning it all—winning the cup, the championship, the title—being the very best in your league and finishing on top. And it is damn tough!

I admit I made some mistakes at MLSE, hiring some rookie general managers; but I thought I had that all figured out when we hired proven winners like Brian Burke and Bryan Colangelo. MLSE spent millions of dollars building practice facilities for the Leafs, Marlies, and TFC. We hired more scouts, more senior front-office managers, and a sports psychologist. We spent all the money that capped leagues would allow us to spend on player salaries. We went "best in class" when it came to travel, dressing rooms, and training. In the Leafs' case, we even brought the Marlies to Toronto at a cost of seven million dollars a year to better develop our young players and for efficient salary cap management. And still we lost.

Brett Brown, former assistant coach of the NBA's San Antonio Spurs and current coach of the Philadelphia 76ers, once said it so well: "To be the last man standing is so ridiculously hard. People have no idea what it is like to play in June." Clearly I never did know what it was like.

In January 2015, I was interviewed by Bob McCown and Elliotte Friedman on Toronto sports-talk radio station Sportsnet 590 The Fan, and they asked me if I had any further insight into winning after being away from MLSE for three years. I told them that I had lots of thoughts on what I would have done differently on the business side of MLSE, but very few on the sports side. That said, I do have two observations.

First, continuity is important. That can be a rare commodity in the world of sports, and sometimes in business. I now believe MLSE (and for that matter most pro teams) are way too quick to fire their coaches. In the NHL, approximately thirty percent of the head coaches get fired every year. In the NBA only six coaches have coached with their existing team for more than four years. In business I absolutely know that you can't have success with this kind of leadership instability, so why are we surprised when we don't have success in sports when we are making frequent changes to personnel?

> **"Continuity in leadership is equally important in business."**

Conversely, Tom Brady of the NFL's New England Patriots has had great success, winning five Super Bowl rings during his long career with the team. Scott Pioli, head of the Patriots' player personnel department, pointed to Brady's long tenure with the team as a key to his and the Patriots' success: "Knowing who the leader is and making sure that people are going to fit with what the leadership wants and how they want to do it . . . stability at the top is crucial to the team's success."

In the case of TFC within the MLSE portfolio, the team's coaching and general management have been a revolving door from the very beginning. We never got it right when I was there. One year the coach was offence-minded. The next coach focused on defence. This lack of consistency trickles down to the players, resulting in confusion and reflecting in their performance on the field.

On the basketball side, the Raptors currently have coaching stability with Dwane Casey, but over their history they have changed coaches every two-and-one-half years since their inception in 1995. Leaf coaches changed only twice when I was with MLSE, but they have now changed four times since I left. In hindsight, I think we pulled the trigger too quickly on getting rid of Pat Quinn, Paul Maurice, Sam Mitchell, and Jay Triano in our hockey and basketball operations. And our TFC coaches were hardly around long enough to even get to know. (Other than Preki—I quickly knew that guy definitely had to go.) And on the subject of Dallas Eakins, former Marlies' head coach in MLSE's minor-league hockey system, I will declare a bias upfront: I also believe the Edmonton Oilers moved way too quickly, letting him go after a grand total of only 113 games.

Continuity in leadership is equally important in business in general. Now granted, decades ago corporations often kept their CEOs on for far too long. But today many organizations are guilty of the same high turnover and instability in the leadership ranks as many sports teams, with the average CEO tenure now less than four years. I believe that a new boss ideally goes through four stages, and this development takes time:

- Year One: Learn the business.
- Year Two: Start throwing a few ideas at the wall to see which ones stick.
- Year Three: Build upon the successes and discard the failures.
- Year Four: Enjoy the results of your efforts.

I can tell you that was the process we essentially followed at Pillsbury, SkyDome, and on the business side of MLSE. Only at MLSE our positive steps three and four lasted over eight successful years.

The second thing that has become clear to me is how really tough it is to play in Toronto (and, by extension, to succeed in any kind of glaring public spotlight). I thought I understood it while I was with MLSE, but now I can objectively see even more clearly. With journalists and columnists from around fifty television and radio stations, newspapers, websites, and official bloggers commenting daily on MLSE—not only in the sports sections, but also in business, lifestyle, and even in the political sections—it is the most public company in Canada. Add to that the fanaticism of fans who are further fuelled by social media, playing in Toronto is often not a lot of fun. For instance, after a long winning streak and during a short losing streak, Dwane Casey had this to say about his players and some supporters:

"We are all happy and full of joy and peanuts and candy when we are winning, but you find out who the real people are when you hit adversity."

Another guy who should know about the challenge of playing and coaching in Toronto is former Leafs coach and current Winnipeg Jets head coach, Paul Maurice. He famously said that the Toronto sports market is like "a drive-by shooting." Former Leaf, Darcy Tucker, summed it all up when he said to me that Toronto is not an easy place to be sure: "But when it's good, it's really good."

So what do I now take away from all this? Hiring the right people is important and incredibly difficult in business and in sports. As far as trading for or signing new players, it is even more difficult in the Toronto market. The team GMs need to take even more time determining whether a player can effectively play, or a coach can effectively coach, in the pressure cooker that is the Toronto market. Tucker reinforced this in a comment he made to the *Toronto Star*: "You have to find the ways and the guys that have the mentality to compete and the desire to win."

When psychologist Dr. Dana Sinclair worked for the Leafs and Raptors, she tested the players for their ability to handle pressure, but did management scouts pay enough attention to her findings? Also, realistically there is no way that MLSE team managers can assemble entire rosters impervious to pressure, so they are absolutely going to have to make sure that they have a few vocal, strong leaders in the dressing room who can help the others survive. Like sports teams, companies also need to have strong leaders thoughout the organization to be successful. If you wish to be one of those leaders your company counts on, you will have to be consistently upping your leadership game.

• • • • •

To help me wrap up this discussion on the challenge of winning as it applies to business and leadership in general, I quote Dr. Noel Tichy from his book, *The Leadership Engine*, in which he talks about the importance of development, continuity, and succession:

> "The answer I have come up with is that winning companies win because they have good leaders who nurture the development of other leaders at all levels of the organization. The ultimate test of success for an organization is not whether it can win today but whether it can keep winning tomorrow and the day after. Therefore, the ultimate test for a leader is not whether he or she makes smart decisions and takes decisive action, but whether he or she teaches others to be leaders and builds an organization that can sustain its success even when he or she is not around."

Like I said, the challenge of "winning it all" is damn tough, whether it be in business or on the playing field. And it's even tougher when you are operating under the bright spotlight of the media and your avid fans . . . or customers.

LESSON 19

BE A COMPLETE COACH

NOW, FOR YOU TO BE A COMPLETE LEADER, you can follow all of the leadership tips in this book, the advice in the other books I have recommended, plus the lessons I have featured from twenty-one proven leaders. You can read all the leadership books in the bookstores and all the articles in the *Harvard Business Review*. You can watch hour after hour of TED Talks. There is no end to the advice you can find on how to be a great twenty-first century leader. But unless you put it all into practice and actually use all this advice to lead others, none of it means very much.

One of the key, practical aspects of being a leader is coaching those who report to you. Helping to maximize the potential of your employees is an enormously important part of your leadership role, and is something you must put into practice every day. However, coaching does not come naturally or easily to many leaders. One way to make this lesson easier is to turn to the world of sports for some instruction.

> **"Helping to maximize the potential of your employees is an enormously important part of your leadership role."**

The practice of leadership, and business in general, are often compared to sports. There are many parallels between these two worlds, and coaching others to be their best is just one of them. I happened to spend a good part of my career at the intersection of business and sports and, in my experience, both aspects of the word "coach" definitely apply to both those spheres: the verb, "to teach and train," as well as the noun, "one who instructs or trains."

I have been lucky enough to see exemplary coaching in action, both in the companies I have led and in the sports coaches that I have observed close up in my years at MLSE. And I took many lessons from the talented sports coaches I've been around. For instance, former Marlies head coach, Dallas Eakins, is a wonderful communicator; his players always know where they stand with him. Pat Quinn commanded respect from, and instilled confidence in, his Leafs. And current Raptors coach, Dwane Casey, is precise about what skills he wants to see his young Raptors develop.

I believe that when all is said and done, the good coaches—in business or in sports—simply excel in three key areas, all of which I cover in leadership lessons elsewhere in this book: clear two-way communications, timely recognition, and careful mentoring.

• • • • •

Interestingly enough, when I teach at the Odette School of Business, I often ask the students to describe the traits of both good and bad coaches or leaders. Surprisingly, they seem collectively to get it pretty right, thanks in part to their experience with part-time jobs or playing on sports teams. So I tell them that they already know how to be a good coach and clearly do not require any leadership training, and joke that they should be able to leave the class immediately. But we all know that being a great leader is not that easy.

In fact, there are too many leaders who don't even care to coach others, or who are too into themselves to even realize how bad at it they are; bad coaches are all too common. The psychopaths who use threats and hard tactics with little concern for the company's values. The "enough about me what do you think about me?" narcissists who feel they are so special and love only their own ideas. Years ago when I took a YPO (young presidents organization under forty) leadership course, I did not recognize any psychopaths in the room, but I sure did recognize a few young presidents who thought they had little to learn about being better.

> **"Good coaching is not easy and doesn't always come naturally."**

And this long quote from educator Robert Donmoyer summarizes perfectly how tough it is to be a complete coach. Pointedly, his quote stresses that there are no time-outs if you want to be that consistently complete leader and coach:

> "Employees are ever alert for signs of competence, vision and trustworthiness in their leaders. When they see these positive signs, they work harder, contribute better ideas and stay with the company longer. When they pick up unsettling signals their performance and loyalty deteriorate. Because the scrutiny and interpretation are relentless, even trivial things that you say have an impact. For a leader, there's no such thing as a casual conversation. You can't manage the signals that you send. Even if your intentions are pure and your performance flawless, don't be surprised when your most innocuous statements are assigned deep, sinister meaning—or are assigned very different meanings by different people. But if you communicate consistently and clearly, especially in times of crisis and don't shy

away from the tough issues, you'll engender the trust and confidence that you need to succeed."

Dee Hock, the founder of the Visa credit card, boiled the essence of leadership down to a very simple sort of one-minute leadership Ph.D.: "Make a careful list of all things done to you that you abhorred. Don't do them to others, ever. Make another list of the things done for you that you loved. Do them to others, always." Again, pretty clear and pretty effective. But perhaps still a little too simple. Or not quite complete.

• • ● • •

The secret to being a complete, successful leader is putting all of this advice to work to lead others. And coaching is an important key to helping your employees improve continuously to maximize their potential. But ask any business leader or any sports coach and they will tell you that good coaching is not easy and doesn't always come naturally. Being a successful coach who is on top of their game all the time is impossible. Business pressures, personal pressures, too much work, too little time, changing markets, new competitors, and so on, and so on—the unending litany of daily challenges causes even the best leaders to slip up on helping others along.

At the risk of being redundant, there are essentially three key skills that are extremely important to develop if you want to be a complete coach:

- Clear, complete, timely (and often repetitive) two-way communications. Listen as much as you talk.

- Catch your people in the act of doing something good and give them positive, specific recognition. Say thanks frequently, creatively, and sincerely.
- Recognize that being a mentor, coach, and developer of talent is an important part of your job. Only by carefully relating to the unique strengths and development needs of your individual employees will you get through to them and make a positive difference in their performance.

Again, to succeed as a leader you need to be a complete coach. That means constantly communicating, recognizing, and helping your people develop. All against a backdrop of constant scrutiny and sometimes unfair criticism.

> **“Coaching is an unending task and a very tough job—there are no time-outs.”**

Sorry, if you thought getting a degree, reading leadership books, and getting promoted was enough to make you an effective leader, you are mistaken. Great leadership also requires that you be a great coach. That's an unending task and a very tough job—there are no time-outs. The good news is that helping your employees improve through your everyday coaching can be one of the most rewarding aspects of your role as a leader.

LESSON 20

BE A BUILDER: ADD BRICKS TO THE CIVIL FOUNDATION

"A society grows great when old men plant trees whose shade they know they shall never sit in." —*Old Greek proverb*

THE CONCEPT OF ADDING BRICKS to the civil foundation came to me when I read Roger Martin's book, *Fixing the Game: Bubbles, Crashes, and What Capitalism Can Learn from the NFL.* When I set out to read his book I imagined I was going to read about how to fix Bay Street and Wall Street using a football analogy. Surprisingly, the most impactful idea I took from Martin's book was the important role corporations and individuals need to play in society: "The people who run these companies have a choice: they can chip away at the bricks of the civil foundation; they can benefit from the existing foundation, but not contribute to it; or they can work to add bricks to strengthen the robustness of the foundation." During my career I realized that I wanted to add bricks and make communities better. I also realized that doing that also made me a much better leader.

"Corporations and individuals need to play an important role in society."

Personally, I have enjoyed a history of actively giving back money and time to various causes and institutions, stretching back to my late twenties. I have helped institutions like the University of Windsor, United Way, Children's Aid Society, Toronto Wildlife Centre, PetSmart Charities, and many others. When I retired, my wife, Colleen, and I started our own foundation, focusing on initiatives targeted at inner-city youth.

My contributions are not nearly as great as philanthropists like the late Joe Rotman or Ted Rogers, nor the still very active civic leaders like Allan Slaight, or Larry and Judy Tanenbaum; but I still know I have done my part. And while I led MLSE I was really proud of the fact that I helped the company invest over one billion dollars in important community infrastructure like arenas and stadiums.

Okay but why have I included "add bricks to the civil foundation" as one of my leadership lessons? Because, as a leader, your personal return on civil investment in the community will be immense. You will get to work with diverse teams of people that are outside your comfort zone. You will build a much larger network. So many times the people I worked with on charitable boards popped up later in my corporate life. You will learn things. You will help build important things. You will feel proud and even have some fun. And, yes, all of this will make you more well rounded, empathetic, and a smarter leader.

• • • • •

Since retiring I know my outlook on "adding bricks" has changed. I have become a more aggressive advocate for social issues that are important to me. So much so that, much to the surprise of many of my friends, I supported longtime NDPer Olivia Chow in her campaign for mayor of Toronto. I have voiced my opinion on questionable transit decisions like the Scarborough subway; I have spoken out against racism, and jets using the Billy Bishop airport; and I have clearly endorsed the belief that humans are the primary cause of climate change. I started to wonder out loud if my beliefs were becoming too left wing.

One day over breakfast, I met with the talented and incredibly committed councillor of Toronto's Ward 27, Kristyn

Wong-Tam. I said to Kristyn, "My problem is that I don't believe I'm left wing . . . fiscally responsible and socially liberal, yes; but not left wing." Kristyn replied, "Richard, you are not left wing, you are progressive." I looked up the definition of "progressive" and it talked about "using or interested in new or modern ideas, especially in politics and education." I took the *Toronto Star* Political Sentimeter survey, which measures ideological types of some 60,000 Torontonians, and tested the same as twenty-five percent of the city: "Social Democrat Left." People who fit this profile are characterized as follows: "embrace diversity, a strong advocate for social and economic equality." And you know I am good with this assessment of my values. I can live comfortably with being a progressive.

• • • • •

If I were still president of MLSE, I suspect that today I would be a different kind of president, leading more with heart than I once did. And as much as MLSE was a great corporate citizen and city builder, I would try to get them to do even more. Today there is so much solid rationale for leaders and companies to be more socially responsible and to proactively develop strategies that foster corporate social responsibility (CSR).

I strongly believe that businesses today must have concrete CSR strategies. Not just half-hearted window dressing, but strategies that align with the company's values and are coordinated across the enterprise. For example, I really like how CEO Tim Cook has brought philanthropy back to Apple. At a shareholders'

"I believe that as a leader you need to speak up on social matters."

meeting in early 2015, the National Center for Public Policy Research (NCPPR) wanted Apple to commit right then and there to doing only those things that were profitable. Cook's response was passionate and uncharacteristically blunt: "When we work on making our devices accessible to the blind, I don't consider the bloody ROI." He also went on to tell them, "If you want me to do things for only ROI reasons you should get out of this stock." Now, I know he said all that after the latest quarterly financial results had been released in December 2014, announcing that Apple earnings had grown forty-eight percent to a record eighteen billion dollars, but his stance was impressive just the same.

Admittedly, Apple's recent financial performance makes Cook a pretty bulletproof executive right now, but you have to love his spunk. On top of Cook's declarations in early 2015, he has announced that he plans to donate his $785 million personal fortune to charity with this explanation: "You want to be the pebble in the pond that creates the ripples for change."

I wish more leaders would be this generous and also stand up to the business critics who are calling out for slashing headcount and closing plants, actions that only fluff up short-term financial results and harm the company and its community long-term. Closer to home, I was impressed with Scotiabank's 2014 Corporate Social Responsibility Report. The document is incredibly comprehensive and embraces everything from its employees to its marketplace, community, and the environment.

I believe that as a leader you need to speak up on social matters. At the height of the media frenzy surrounding the mayor Rob Ford scandals, the *Toronto Star* asked community leaders their thoughts on his behaviour. Some leaders, such as Richard Florida, renowned urban studies thinker and Rotman professor, and Toronto Foundation CEO, Rahul Bhardwaj, agreed to speak up. Disappointingly, leaders like Rob Pritchard, CEO of Metrolinx, Indigo CEO, Heather Reisman, and too many others declined to speak out against Ford's antics. I applaud leaders and organizations that speak up on important community and national issues; and I think that the ones that do not are missing an opportunity to contribute to meaningful dialogue.

"Socially responsible companies increase their employees' motivation, energy, and engagement."

Today, socially engaged leaders such as Starbucks founder and CEO, Howard Schultz, are going against the normal CEO grain and speaking up on everything from guns to gay rights. As Schultz puts it, "Doing what is right for society and doing what is right for business cannot be mutually exclusive endeavors. While it is always safer to stand on the sidelines, that is not leadership. Today, we choose to act in a way that is authentic to us, by nurturing a sense of community and bringing people together."

• • • • •

Aside from doing good as an individual and as an organization, there are other benefits to be gained from being socially responsible. For example, potential and existing employees will be attracted to a leader and a company that is more socially responsible. There is plenty of research to support that socially responsible companies increase their employees' motivation, energy, and engagement.

And going one step further, actively including your employees in the corporate CSR strategies allows them to contribute both at the office and outside it. As part of our MLSE Foundation, we refurbished old neighbourhood ice rinks and basketball courts. With each of these projects we undertook, we asked our employees if they wanted to volunteer their time to participate in the renovations, and every time more employees than we needed signed up. Not only did these employees enjoy participating in a team event out of the office, they were proud that they were giving back to communities that needed their help. They liked what MLSE was doing and it reinforced in me that companies that have a greater purpose are viewed as a better place to work.

So the lesson I want to impart in this chapter is for you to get involved, to give back, and as a leader add bricks to the civil foundation. Over the years, three of Toronto's biggest social activists realized that the three levels of government combined could not do it all for the city. So they each stepped up, literally and figuratively helping to build a better city, a city that works and supports its citizens. Their names were David Pecaut, June Callwood, and Jane Jacobs. For you to surpass or even match their contributions will be very difficult, but if you at least try, you will be a much better and a more authentic leader.

The power of a person like you to make a change is significant. In today's world, with so many local and international challenges, standing still is simply not an option for you. And if you require more convincing, remember Winston Churchill's quote, "We make a living by what we get, but we make a life by what we give."

LESSON 21

GET BACK TO THE GYM

"THE GREATEST GLORY IN LIVING lies not in never failing but in rising up every time we fail." That from Nelson Mandela, who always got back up from incredible hardship very few, if any of us, will ever experience.

In today's incredibly fast moving, complex, and competitive world, you can be an outstanding leader and still fail. Sometimes it will be because you made a basic mistake as a leader, and that caused you to get fired. Maybe because you have some bad personal values and they finally caught up with you. Or you could be a victim of a merger, a takeover, or a corporate downsizing. During your career, be prepared to be let go from your job a couple of times. It is the new business norm in the twenty-first century. Clearly, during your career you will need a gym bag full of leadership lessons to draw from if you want to do more than survive—if you want to flourish.

During my life and career, I had a number of setbacks. My very first one was the high-school guidance councillor telling me that I was of only average intelligence and she had no clue what career direction I should take. My second stumbling block came at the end of grade twelve. I wished to enter a special program at the university called preliminary year, but my marks were not good enough to get accepted. I took the initiative to meet with my high-school principal and he increased my grade point average just enough to get me out of high school and into the University of Windsor. On reflection, I think both of those high-school experiences had a lasting psychological impact on my life. I needed

> **"Take the time to reflect upon failure and turn it into wisdom."**

to prove to people that I had potential. Perseverance went in my gym bag.

My third obstacle was being passed over for promotion to brand manager at Colgate, while all but one of my peers were promoted. Six months later I, too, was promoted and immediately commenced a fast track through marketing at Colgate and General Foods. When I was thirty-three, I lost out in my bid for the president's role at Mattel toys. Two years later I was president of Hostess Foods and, in hindsight, much more ready for the president's role at that point. Preparation went into my gym bag.

However, easily my greatest setback was when the group I was part of lost their bid for the Toronto NBA franchise. Our team, the Palestra group—consisting of Labatt Breweries, Larry Tanenbaum, Paul Beeston, Jack Donohue, and myself—were the prohibitive favourites, but we lost to the Slaight-Bitove group nonetheless. It is said that lack of success at crucial moments in your life can sometimes prove invaluable later on, however frustrating it might seem at the time. I now believe that to be true, especially if one takes the time to reflect upon the failure and turn it into wisdom.

The NBA setback was an especially painful one for me, because I had fallen just short of realizing my then twenty-three-year dream of running a basketball team. I was so very close, but we screwed up and we lost. The day after the announcement, I read an article in the paper about a businessman who had lost out on purchasing a company he very much wanted. He lost in a bitter public fight and it was a great disappointment to him. But instead of giving up and being depressed, he said something that really resonated with me and helped me get over my NBA defeat: "They won . . . I lost . . . next!" The importance of having a dream definitely stayed in my gym bag.

I took his remarks to heart and my "next" was president and COO of Labatt Communications, the broadcast company that controlled TSN, RDS, Dome Productions, and The Discovery Channel. The company soon became NetStar, when a partnership group of ESPN, Reitmans, plus Stephen Bronfman's company, Claridge, completed a management-led leveraged buyout of Labatt's broadcast assets.

As it turned out, NetStar was a perfect place for me to learn from television experts and a chance to report to a Canadian broadcast icon, Gordon Craig. Plus I owned a small piece of the company and had dreams of some day making millions when we either sold NetStar or issued an IPO. Fortuitously, I was also learning a lot about sports broadcasting and digital media, which turned out to be critical when Allan Slaight approached me to be the president of the Raptors three years later. Getting my ticket punched stayed in my gym bag.

"No matter how good a leader you are, your career will not always be smooth sailing."

During your career, you will surely have setbacks and often you will fail. No matter how good a leader you are, your career will not always be smooth sailing. The key will be how you get back up. In basketball, when your fitness is low, your jump shot is not falling, and the team is losing, the great players step up. As Dwane Casey said after a bad loss to Atlanta, "We are in a rut and the only way we are going to get out of it is to work our way out." In other words, if you experience a career setback, don't make excuses. Pick up your leadership gym bag and get back to the gym. And, of course, think, "Next!"

BONUS!

21 OF MY OWN QUOTABLE QUOTES

I HAVE USED A NUMBER OF EXPRESSIONS or quotes in my everyday business conversations over the years. Some of the quotes came from people I worked with, while others came from books, newspaper articles, or even movies. And in some cases I think I actually made them up myself. In coming up with ideas for this book, I thought it might be fun to list twenty-one of these things I used to say on a regular basis.

To help me remember them, I reached out to my senior MLSE management team for examples and they all weighed in quickly and enthusiastically. It turns out that Robin Brudner has an incredible memory and remembered over half of the quotes that appear here. Again, I have provided a backstory to each of them to give you some context.

I have put all of them in "quotes" because I am sure that some are from writers, but over time I have just forgotten who they were. I hope they will forgive me.

• • • • •

1: "GROSS IS NOT THE NET."

This quote absolutely has to be the number one expression I am associated with. To teach senior MLSE managers the importance of growing or protecting both percentage and dollar margins, I started carrying a wooden sign to meetings with this quote carved on it. After much explanation and constant reminders, pretty much everyone got the message and the positive impact on the company's bottom line was noticeable. When I retired, the employees handed out 700 Richard Peddie bobbleheads they had commissioned, with my likeness holding a sign that read, "The gross is not the net."

2: "CRAZY-ASS IDEA OF THE WEEK."

About once a week, usually on a Saturday morning, I would send out an idea to a group of employees. The idea could have been about food and beverage, game operations, new products—anything. I knew that not all of the ideas were that good, but I wanted people to at least think about them. And then either discard them, build upon them, or adopt them. My hope was that my early morning email would get others to think creatively and come up with their own "crazy-ass" ideas to grow the company.

3: "THE HOT DOGS DON'T TASTE AS GOOD WHEN YOU ARE LOSING."

At Air Canada Centre, we always used the same hot dog and the same hot dog bun supplier. We grilled them the same way every time. And we always supplied the same wide choice of condiments. When Brian Burke was the Leaf president, we even had "Burkie's Dog House," and every night the line up of fans waiting for a dog was very long. So our hot dogs were predictably good. However, when our teams were losing it was also predictable that some fans would express their unhappiness by complaining that our hot dogs didn't taste as good. Who knew that a losing team would negatively impact how the taste of our hot dogs was perceived?

4: "THAT DOG WON'T HUNT."

When the Leafs bought the Raptors, I had to go to Montreal and meet with the Air Canada president to talk about the value of the naming rights deal for our arena. When the naming rights agreement was originally negotiated, we imagined that the arena would host only the Raptors, concerts, and family shows. Obviously, having the Leafs as a tenant would dramatically increase the title exposure of the building, so my job was to convince Lamar Durrett that Air Canada needed to significantly increase their dollar investment on the sponsorship.

When I first pitched the idea to him, he said to me in his personable, southern drawl, "Richard, that dog won't hunt." Now, I did not like his answer, but I sure loved his quote. Eventually Air Canada did increase their investment in the naming rights, but even with the increased level of sponsorship, they got one hell of a twenty-year bargain. When Air Canada went into bankruptcy years later, I talked to then Air Canada president, Robert Milton, and asked him if he wanted to get out of the deal. I was hoping to sell the arena title to someone else for a much higher price. Recognizing how good the titling deal was, however, Robert passed. It will be interesting to see if Air Canada renews its title deal in 2019.

5: "WE SHOT THE BEAR—AND NOW WE HAVE TO GET IT OUT OF THE WOODS."

I am not a hunter and I could never, ever shoot a bear, but I do know that they can weigh up to 600 pounds. So while it is one thing to shoot a bear, it is another thing to carry it out of the woods.

Sometimes the companies I led decided to invest in new initiatives that we knew were good, but that we also knew would take a lot of effort to make successful. Two good examples at MLSE were Toronto FC and our entry into specialty television. Professional football (remember, I don't call it soccer) had failed numerous times in Toronto before TFC. In 2006 the price for a Major League Soccer franchise was a low $10 million U.S. (today the league average is $157 million); but we also had to build a stadium, sell thousands of tickets, attract major sponsors, and build a good product on the pitch. We got the "TFC bear" out of the woods by doing all those things very well, except for the last one.

In the case of Raptors TV and Leafs TV, the entry cost was low but we had no broadcast facilities, no broadcast staff, and no carriage deals with Rogers or Bell. Nonetheless, a good team, led by John Shannon and Tom Anselmi, got both channels up and running. Later, Chris Hebb and his team got them running very well. Years later, our entry into broadcast was instrumental in Ontario Teachers' Pension Plan selling MLSE for an enterprise value of two billion dollars. I continue to believe that price was a steal. Today, MLSE must be worth closer to four billion dollars than two billion.

6: "LONG RUN FOR A SHORT SLIDE."

I have always liked this expression. It's a very concise, pithy way of saying that sometimes it takes a lot of work and a lot of time to get something done, and when you get there it's not worth all the effort. For instance, we looked at buying the Argos twice when I was president, and I recommended that we pass both times. In both cases we thought it would require a lot of work and effort to get fans and sponsors interested in the Argos again. And even if we did succeed, the operating profit would be less than a million dollars a year (approximately one percent of MLSE profits); therefore, owning the Argos would not move the dial on MLSE's enterprise value at all.

7: "HIRE FOR ATTITUDE; TRAIN FOR SKILL."

The service industry is a different beast. The customer (or in MLSE's case, the fan) is right in front of you or on the other end of the phone line. Not everyone has the emotional make up to always be friendly, helpful, or calm when things are going wrong. Accordingly, we looked for new employees who had the right attitude and we figured we could train them for the skills they needed. We also figured that having high enthusiasm for the job was a prerequisite.

When we staffed up for the opening of Air Canada Centre, we had to hire a lot of new employees. Sure, we could read their résumé and interview them; but what did that tell us about their energy level, creativity, and enthusiasm? So we tried something new. All of the candidates had to act out something. Our hundreds of applicants were game, enthusiastically acting out some very entertaining skits. As it turned out, the movie *Titanic* was a popular choice. Job applicant after applicant sang "My Heart Will Go On," by Celine Dion. Due to their sheer enthusiasm and courage most of them got hired.

8: "UNDER PROMISE; OVER DELIVER."

When we ran MLSE, we had to go before the board to get approval for our annual fiscal plan, capital expenditures, and key strategies. Our recommended objectives were never easy. In fact they were always aggressive, which was borne out in the dramatic increase in enterprise value in my time as president. However, at the same time, we tried to leave a little bit in reserve when it came to revenue targets or timelines. This worked well for a while, but then Larry Tanenbaum caught on to our tricks and started pushing us for even higher targets.

9: "HIRE SLOWLY; FIRE QUICKLY."

You hear this expression a lot today and I think it has real merit. At MLSE we would get job applications from over 20,000 people a year. Working at MLSE was a dream job for many. So we had the luxury of picking from a lot of excellent applicants. Accordingly, we had to resist the tendency to rush, and instead take our time with interviewing, testing, and even having the final two lead candidates make formal presentations.

By "fire quickly" I do not mean cold, hurried firings. Instead, we believed in written evaluations that identified any development needs the individual had to work on. However, if the development needs persisted, the individual would get a "needs improvement." Sometimes these "needs improvements" went on too long and we did not let the person go as quickly as we should have. On the other hand, as I wrote in Lesson 18, I do not believe sports teams should fire coaches so quickly, but rather give the coaches time to develop their players into a winning team.

10: "ON A BAD TEAM SOMEONE HAD TO SCORE SOME POINTS."

I learned this when the Raptors traded for Lamond Murray. Murray was a leading performer for a bad Cleveland Cavaliers team, averaging sixteen points and five boards per game. With the Raptors, his stats dropped to six and two. Often, fans and team management can get sucked into thinking that the player is good, instead of just a player who is taking all the shots. A classic case of the good stats/bad team phenomenon. With the new focus on analytics, this shouldn't be happening as often in pro sports today. But it could just as easily be happening in your business. Beware of this illusion. Oh, and by the way, Lamond's jersey number was 21.

11: "IF YOU GET THE OBJECTIVES RIGHT, THE STRATEGIES WILL WRITE THEMSELVES."

Not completely true, but pretty true. Unfortunately many people get confused between objectives and strategies. Objectives are *what* you want to achieve in sales, consumer awareness, attitudes, profits, or return on investment, for example. Strategies are *how* you are going to deliver on the objectives, and can involve marketing, sales, people, capital investment plans, and so on. I found that if you really have your employees zero in on a couple of very measurable objectives, then they have a much easier time coming up with the proper strategies.

12: "THE TEAMS ARE THE ENGINES."

Sometimes we got a little full of ourselves on the business side at MLSE. For instance, if the Raptors were playing really well and ticket sales were booming, like they were in the Vince Carter days, we thought we were pretty damn good salespeople. Or, if we looked at the Leafs' league-leading gate revenue, then we thought we must be great marketers. Often a really good salesperson would leave our company for another franchise or facility and learn that maybe they were not quite as good as they thought. They learned that selling a lesser team with not nearly the same level of fan avidity was really a challenge. During your career you may get on a very nice personal roll and start feeling pretty good about yourself. Maybe even too good about yourself, and inflate the contribution you are making. Remember, very seldom is someone bigger than the company, and maybe you have had much of your success because of the company you are working for or the brand you were working on.

13: "YOU HIRE STRANGERS AND FIRE FRIENDS."

Once you have let someone go who has worked for you for years, this saying hits very close to home. More often than not, you hire someone you don't know. Over time you meet their family, celebrate successes over a few beers, maybe play a little golf together, and you get to be friends. But often the company changes and the individual is having trouble keeping up. So for the overall good of the organization he or she has to go. It's the right move, but it's never easy to fire a friend.

14: "RUNNING OUT OF RUNWAY."

I first heard former NBA commissioner, David Stern, use this term at a board of governors meeting. He was talking about his belief that the NBA had to come up with new revenue streams because the current ones were starting to max out. I liked the expression because we also had similar concerns with some of our existing MLSE revenue lines. Knowing that we had to continue to grow revenue got us into TFC, television networks, and our Maple Leaf Square investments.

15: "IT'S NOT BRAGGING IF YOU CAN DO IT."

When CFO Ian Clarke and I were putting together the bank syndicate to cover MLSE's original debt financing, we had almost no operating history. We could only guesstimate what our revenues and expenses might be. To be able to secure millions of dollars of debt financing, we had to commit to high levels of contractually obligated income (long-term sponsorships, broadcast deals, suite agreements, etc.). We also had to agree to meet some very specific ratios like debt service coverage (operating profit to cover interest payments) and a leverage ratio (debt to EBITDA), or we would be offside with our lenders. And if that happened, it would give our lenders the ability to hit us with some pretty expensive financial penalties.

As it turned out, we achieved our revenue and profit targets quite comfortably and we were always safely within our covenants. Ian and I were pretty proud of MLSE's financial results and we actually started off one lender presentation with the headline, "It's not bragging if you can do it." That was the quote we used years ago; if I were doing the same presentation today, I would quote Bruno Mars's hit song, "Uptown Funk," and use his lyrics, "Don't believe me, just watch."

16: "MANAGERS MANAGE WHAT HAS ALREADY BEEN CREATED; LEADERS CREATE SOMETHING NEW."

Some people are only ever going to be managers. They can run an existing business and often keep it operating satisfactorily for a long time. But try to give them a role where they have to be a leader and create new initiatives, then they are in trouble. I always liked having some competent managers; but for any company to grow, it needs a lot of excellent leaders.

17: "I CAN FIND A LOT OF PEOPLE TO PROJECT LOSSES."

Many of my staff reminded me that I occasionally said this. It usually happened at budget time, when a manager or director brought in a recommended budget that forecast a drop in sales or profits. Now, sometimes there was good reason for such a forecast; but other times the person making the pitch was not being creative, not being bold enough, or did not even know his or her numbers. This quote was not one that people liked hearing from me because it usually meant they were in trouble.

18: "RESPECT FIRST, LOVE SECOND."

When I started out in the consumer products industry, I saw a lot of behaviour that put "love" first and "respect" second. By that I mean that our company leaders would seldom make sales calls, but would instead try to win over a client by taking them out for dinner, inviting them out for a round of golf, or taking them to a Leafs game. I found that behaviour not to be authentic, and I was personally uncomfortable doing it.

At Pillsbury I decided to do something quite the opposite. I seldom took our customers to a social event. Instead I made sure that every year I called on them at their offices and presented an action plan that would grow their business. One year the presentation was called, "Grow with the (Green) Giant." Another year it was, "Popping Fresh Ideas from Pillsbury." In almost all cases, the presentation was a success and our sales with the account took off. Attitudes towards Pillsbury changed dramatically, and in turn I became friends with the presidents of Loblaws, Sobey's, and A&P whom I called on. In the end, the action plans helped their businesses and gained us their respect. I found that the presentations were much more effective than a steak dinner and tickets to a game. Ironic that seven years later I would run MLSE, which counts on a lot of businesses entertaining their clients at our games.

19: "SERVICE SELLS AND SERVICE RESELLS."

Many would say that the twenty-first century is a service century. With immediate free delivery, twenty-four-hour help lines, money-back guarantees, and the like, companies are trying to get ahead of their competitors by offering better service. Naturally, offering up great service is one of the reasons for someone to purchase your product. But as we all know, sometimes that service promise is all hot air. From my experience, if you live up to your promise and really deliver great service, it will help you retain customers and probably even help up-sell them.

20: "ONE SWALLOW DOESN'T MAKE A SUMMER."

Sometimes a false spring comes to my house on Boblo Island and an occasional tree swallow or barn swallow shows up weeks too early. I worry about their survival because they count on flying insects, and when the weather turns cold again, the insects are nowhere to be found. Just as one swallow doesn't mean it's summer, often early sales or market research trends can be very misleading. Don't jump to conclusions before claiming victory.

21: AND, FINALLY: "EXCELLENT!"

If you ask me how I am, you will invariably hear me say, "Excellent!" A lot of people today say, "Not bad," which I think is a completely nonsensical response! "Not bad?" What exactly does that even mean?

Your employees or your team members continually look to you as their leader for an indication of how things are going. If your response is any of, "I am ok . . . tired . . . lousy . . . wish sales were better . . . not bad," what should they think? So, being mindful of my thoughts on optimism in Lesson 14, that is, "Employee scrutiny and interpretation are relentless," always say, "Excellent!" when asked how you are.

And be sure to ask me how I am when you see me!

• • • • •

So that's my bonus chapter. Some of the quotes may seem frivolous to you, but if you read each backstory and the quote itself carefully, you will see they all reflect a key lesson learned and are lessons that I applied frequently when I was president, leading many different companies. I hope you liked some of these quotes. If they strike your fancy, please free to adopt them and use them as your own.

WRAP UP

ALWAYS KEEP YOUR GYM BAG HANDY

MY PERSONAL NARRATIVE IS ALL HERE in the pages of *21 Leadership Lessons.* It's the story of how I learned what to pack in my leadership gym bag in order to be successful. And I hope some of the lessons I learned—many of them the hard way—and sometimes relearned, will serve you well on your own leadership journey.

If you have stuck with me this far, you have read, by my count, over 100 leadership tips, quotes, and recommended books. In other words, an absolutely crazy amount of leadership advice. When I was a vice president at General Foods, I learned that if I gave my salesforce more than about four things to think about at once, I confused the hell out of them. So why would I give you so many tips? Well because you don't have to read or even pay attention to all of them right now.

My hope is that my *21 Leadership Lessons* can be in your leadership gym bag throughout your entire career. As you move through the many years to come, you will come across many new opportunities, issues, and challenges. You will also evolve as a leader. So tips that you discard, or that don't seem relevant today, may be helpful five or ten years from now.

You clearly have some leadership beliefs of your own right now, and an interest in being a better leader, or you would not even have been interested in reading this book. That's excellent, because over the years you will need to change and grow in your role. When I took over as president of Pillsbury in 1985, I had a personal leadership template that I believed would work and I was keen to try it out. Thankfully it worked very well then, and in my subsequent leadership roles, until 2001.

During the summer of that year, I created the leadership course I was to teach in the fall at the Odette School of Business. In writing the course, I realized that I had not fully kept up with the times and needed to make some adjustments to my leadership style and practice. I needed to put new leadership lessons in my own gym bag. As the head of the Institute of Management Consultants, Jim Thomson, once said, "Leadership in general isn't a point in time or an end state . . . it's a continuum of experience, skills, and always reaching beyond your current set of belief systems and experiences."

They say that one of the best ways to learn is to teach. And learn I did, teaching a semester at Odette and then during my Elite Training classes at MLSE. I also must say that one learns a lot from writing books. Writing *Dream Job* and now *21 Leadership Lessons*, I had to really sharpen, as Tichy would say, my teachable points of view. I have also learned that I could not maintain a high level of leadership skill unless I was a perpetual student of leadership. Now at sixty-eight years of age, I am definitely still learning and far from being a perfect leader.

These days I often start a leadership lecture to students with these statements: "Some of you will grow up to become horrible leaders [then I pause for effect] . . . others of you will become good leaders [another pause] . . . some of you will become great leaders . . . but if you really, really dedicate yourself to being a student of leadership, a few of you can be exceptional leaders. Which one do you want to be?"

Invest, be self-aware, be resilient. Realize that being a great leader is a lifelong journey and, by all means, keep your leadership gym bag handy.

EPILOGUE

AS YOU CAN SEE, THROUGHOUT THIS BOOK I really encourage you to get as much experience as you can—to get your ticket punched to help you realize your dream. The late Steve Jobs called it something different. He called it "connecting the dots:"

> "You have to know that the dots will somehow connect in your future. You have to trust in something—your gut, destiny, life, Karma, whatever. This approach never let me down, and it has made all the difference in my life."
>
> —*Steve Jobs*

At the same time Stephen King is a little skeptical about connecting the dots and wonders if there is a plan for us all:

> "When we look back, we think our lives form patterns; every event starts to look logical, as if something—or someone—has mapped out all our steps (and missteps?) . . . . Once upon a time, I would have said we choose our paths at random: this happened, then that, hence the other. Now I know better."
>
> —*Stephen King*, Revival

Whichever of them is correct, I know with confidence that having a dream, working hard, and always striving to be an authentic, truthful leader will bring you more career and personal success.

ACKNOWLEDGEMENTS

Self-publishing is a unique challenge compared with having a top-notch publishing company like HarperCollins making sure your book gets finished and distributed in bookstores and online. However, I was very lucky to find a special team of individuals who helped make the self-publishing process fun while getting me over the goal line. A special thanks to my editor, Karen Milner, of Milner & Associates, for her patience and her handholding throughout the process. Thank you to Adrian So for his great design work on the book cover and his creative approach to the interior design of the book. Also thanks to Rob Dawson of Georgetown Publications for getting *21 Leadership Lessons* listed in bookstores across Canada. Thanks to Daniella Gullo and Thomas Shadoff for creating a unique social media campaign to raise awareness of the book with young leaders. And, of course, I also need to thank my twenty-one friends who contributed their own important leadership tips. All of them are great leaders in business, sports, or the community.

My most special thanks goes to my wife, Colleen, for her constant encouragement and for her patient explanation of all things computer.

Thank you all.

INDEX

Y

Z

ABOUT THE AUTHOR

Richard Peddie's entire life has been about leading with strong core values and creating enterprise value.

Whether as president of Hostess, Pillsbury, SkyDome, NetStar, or Maple Leaf Sports & Entertainment, he always delivered tremendous financial value to those companies by having a clear leadership vision and consistently practicing strong core values.

A graduate of the University of Windsor business school (today the Odette School of Business), he joined Colgate in sales and marketing. He then moved on to General Foods (today Kraft Foods), where he moved rapidly through their marketing department and became a vice president at twenty-nine years of age. He then became president of GF's Hostess Foods division. In 1985 he left Hostess to become the president and CEO of Pillsbury Canada, where during his tenure the company generated record growth and was recognized as one of Canada's "100 Best Companies." Peddie also received the Donald B. McCaskill Award for Marketing Excellence in Canada for his successful marketing strategies and strong business results while at Pillsbury.

In 1989, after nineteen years in consumer products, Peddie accepted the position of president and CEO of the SkyDome (today the Rogers Centre). During his four years there he helped host more than 1,000 events and entertain almost 30 million guests. SkyDome was chosen as the North American Stadium of the Year for four consecutive years and Peddie was honoured as the North American Facility Manager of the Year in 1992. While at SkyDome, Peddie teamed up with Larry Tanenbaum and applied for an NBA franchise for Toronto. Their application resulted in the NBA coming to Canada, but they lost out on their bid for the franchise to a competing group.

Peddie then became president and COO of NetStar Communications (TSN, RDS, Discovery Channel). In July 1995, he was one of the key individuals in a management-led consortium that purchased the company. While at NetStar he launched Canada's first sports website, TSN.ca.

In late 1996, Peddie was named president and CEO of the Toronto Raptors, thus fulfilling his dream to one day run a basketball team, a dream that he first had while at the University of Windsor in the late 1960s. In 1998, the Maple Leafs bought the Raptors and created Maple Leaf Sports & Entertainment, with Peddie as president and CEO.

Richard was president and CEO of MLSE for fourteen very busy years. From building Air Canada Centre; launching Leafs TV, Raptors TV, and buying Gol TV; to bringing Major League Soccer to Canada and launching TFC; to building the $500 million Maple Leaf Square; Peddie helped grow the company from an enterprise value of $300 million to $2 billion. He did this by consistently practicing four core values: excite every fan, inspire our people, dedicated to our teams, and being leaders in the community.

A proud native of Windsor, Ontario, Peddie graduated from the University of Windsor in 1970 and received an honorary doctorate from the institution in 2001. Today Dr. Peddie is actively involved in the Richard Peddie Leadership Initiative at Odette, where he helps the school successfully create twenty-first century leaders. He is on the board of Alarm Force Industries Inc. and The Toronto Foundation. He is the author of a bestselling book on leadership, entitled *Dream Job*.

• • • • •

I invite you to follow me on Twitter @RichardAPeddie
and at RichardPeddie.com

Drop me a line—I would love to hear your thoughts on leadership.